THE ART OF COMMAND

This guide to the proper use and patterns of language is an excellent tool for flawless results. Written by an authority on language, *TheOne-MinuteGrammarian* is organized like an index—alphabetically—so that you can find the correct entry you need quickly, and get on with the task at hand. If you're looking for the proper spelling of an often misspelled word . . . or need to know the distinct meaning and usage of another word . . . if you want to distinguish the shades of meaning between *anywhere* and *anyplace* . . . even if you want to find out the difference between an adjective and an adjective phrase—this handy, comprehensive book will give you the answers you need and help you to become the most effective writer possible.

MORTON S. FREEMAN is the author of *Words to the Wise: The Wordwatcher's Guide to Contemporary Style and Usage* (Meridian) and former Director of Publications, American Law Institute-American Bar Association. He also writes the "Word Watcher" column, syndicated in the *Philadelphia Inquirer, St. Louis Post-Dispatch, Buffalo News* and other newspapers.

THE ONE-MINUTE GRAMMARIAN

by

Morton S. Freeman

Foreword by S. I. Hayakawa

A SIGNET BOOK

SIGNET
Published by the Penguin Group
Penguin Books USA Inc., 375 Hudson Street,
New York, New York 10014, U.S.A.
Penguin Books Ltd, 27 Wrights Lane,
London W8 5TZ, England
Penguin Books Australia Ltd, Ringwood,
Victoria, Australia
Penguin Books Canada Ltd, 10 Alcorn Avenue,
Toronto, Ontario, Canada M4V 3B2
Penguin Books (N.Z.) Ltd, 182–190 Wairau Road,
Auckland 10, New Zealand

Penguin Books Ltd, Registered Offices:
Harmondsworth, Middlesex, England

First published by Signet, an imprint of New American Library,
a division of Penguin Books USA Inc.

First Printing, February, 1992
10 9 8 7 6 5 4 3 2 1

 REGISTERED TRADEMARK—MARCA REGISTRADA

Printed in the United States of America

To Chuck Deal,
a young visionary who has encouraged
his older friend to keep
climbing

Foreword

Written language ranks among the great inventions of humanity. By reading, we can learn from someone who lived hundreds or even thousands of years ago. Our writing may be read by others across the city, beyond the ocean, or even far into the future. When we put words on paper, we usually do so in the hope that others understand what we are saying.

How do readers understand writing? Linguists, semanticists, and philosophers have spent much effort attempting to describe how readers and listeners interpret language. One important finding is this: Our symbols—spoken and written words—have no innate connection with the things for which they stand. Instead they acquire meaning in our minds by a continuing process of repetition and recognition.

Thus as children we learn language by hearing and imitating the words *soft* or *wet* while touching things that have those qualities. By speaking to others, we learn that "I want apple" is understood more quickly than "Apple want I" and so learn something important about a basic pattern of English sentences.

When we learn to write, we again encounter patterns to master. When we are told that verbs and their subjects should agree in number, or that the meaning of *compose* is different from that of *comprise*, we have been exposed to the formal study of language patterns known as grammar.

Grammar, then, is no more than the study of how language has been used in the past and a guide to its use in the future.

Why does grammar matter? Language is fluid. New words are coined daily. Even some educated speakers these days use *host* as a verb. Nearly everyone says *hopefully* rather than *I hope*, and hardly anyone remembers to use *whom* appropriately. How helpful can yesterday's rules be?

The answers to these questions lie in the nature of our symbolic language. As words have no innate meaning, the most effective writers are those who can understand and control the fine shades of meaning that custom and usage have given them.

Think of a toolbox containing, among other things, a chisel and a screwdriver. We could use the chisel to turn screws and the screwdriver to carve wood, but neither would be perfectly effective. Each would eventually lose its edge, and we would be left with two blunt instruments.

So it is with language. Past speakers of English have found it useful to have, for example, one word, *flout*, that means to mock or to treat with contempt, and another word, *flaunt*, meaning to display vulgarly or immodestly. Use them interchangeably, and both will be dulled. Respect their distinct meanings, and you will be able to flaunt your verbal skills without flouting customary usage.

Think, then, of Morton S. Freeman's new book, *The One-Minute Grammarian*, as an index to the toolbox of language. Mr. Freeman has organized this book like an index, alphabetically, so that a writer may turn to it quickly, find the right tool, and get on with the task at hand.

S.I. Hayakawa
Mill Valley, California

Read this First

Read this First

This book is not the usual kind of grammar that sets out all kinds of technical programs. Quite oppositely, *The One-Minute Grammarian* is designed for the "I-want-an-answer-fast person," for the book is set out in plain English, with brief, direct examples that address many of the grammatical and usage problems that confront most people. This means that you will not have to wade through pages of jargon, diagrams, and complicated explanations. If you want a quick answer, find it merely by getting to it alphabetically. It's as easy as A,B,C.

On thing you can be sure of: *The One-Minute Grammarian* can help give your writing a professional look, simply because what you write will be right!

Please note: A word set in SMALL CAPS means that there's an entry for that word in the text.

A

A is used before words beginning with a consonant sound ("*a* boy," "*a* car"), even though the initial letter may be a vowel ("*a* eulogy," "*a* unit"). **An** is used before words beginning with a vowel sound, regardless of the initial letter ("*an* uncle," "*an* honor"). In contemporary usage *a* predominates over *an* before a sounded *h* ("*a* historic monument," "*a* historical event").

The same principle of sound applies to abbreviations: "*an* FBI agent" (an EFF-B-I agent), "*an* MIT student" (an EM-I-T student), "*a* USSR official."

Do not omit *a* before the second of two singular nouns. Not "I have *a* dictionary and thesaurus," but "*a* dictionary and *a* thesaurus." However, this is not a license to use *a* or *an* superfluously. "What *sort of* [or *what manner of* or *what type of*] man is he?"; not "What sort of *a* man is he?", "What manner of *a* man is he?", and so on.

Remember that when you say, "I have *a* book," it doesn't point to a specific book. To do so, you must use *the*: "I have *the* book."

Able to preferably should not be followed by *to be* (called a *passive infinitive*). Instead of saying, "The bench was not *able to be* repaired because the right material was not delivered," make it "The bench *could not be* repaired because the right material

1

had not been delivered" or "They were not *able to* repair the bench because. . . ."

About is a good short word to mean *approximately*, as in "There were *about* two hundred people there" (prefer *about* to *some* in that example). Except in everyday conversation do not use *about* in the sense of *almost*: "Today is *almost* [not *about*] the warmest day we've had so far"; "We had *almost* [not *about*] reached the crux of the problem when the dean walked in."

Around, which means *encircling*, is more commonly expressed by *about* in the sense of *nearly* or *approximately*: "The fish weighed *about* [not *around*] three pounds." Note that, informally, *around* is widely used to tell time: "They'll meet *around* ten o'clock."

When the sense is *here and there* or *on every side, about* and *around* are interchangeable: "Fred likes to run *about/around*"; "The books were scattered *around/about* the room."

Avoid the combination *at about*. A report might read, "The meeting began at 11 A.M." (precise time) or "about 11 A.M." (approximate time), but not *"at about* 11 A.M." (confused time), even though this last is frequently heard and somewhat established. See ESTIMATED.

Above, meaning *previously mentioned* or *appearing earlier*, as in "the *above* passage," is in common usage, but some writers dislike it. They prefer "the passage *above*," "the passage cited *above*," or, without *above*, "the *preceding* [or *foregoing*] passage." Almost all writers disapprove of *above* when used as a noun. They would avoid "Carefully note the *above.*"

Absolute terms are terms that may not be compared because they are absolute in their own right. For example, *dead* cannot be compared, for nothing can be *more dead* or *the most dead.* If it's dead, it's dead. This simply means that neither *more* nor *most* should precede any of these terms. In addition to *dead,* some other absolutes are *absolute* itself, *complete, equal, eternal, fatal, final, parallel, pregnant, round, supreme, total, unanimous,* and UNIQUE.

Accent marks essential to correct spelling or pronunciation should not be omitted. *Résumé* without the accent marks may be taken to mean *resume,* that is, to begin again, unless the context clearly indicates otherwise. In better writing *fiancé* and *fiancée* without accent marks would be considered misspelled. And so with *cliché, communiqué,* and *façade,* and certainly with proper names, such as *Mendés France.* Note that these marks are used only on words borrowed from foreign languages, primarily French. And note further that stylebooks differ on the use of accent marks. Some would ignore such marks completely.

Accept means *to take, to receive,* or *to agree with.* A person who says yes to someone *accepts.* **Except,** when used as a verb, means *to leave out* or *to exclude.* As a preposition, it means *with the exception of.* "All sophomores were *excepted*" means they were *excluded.* "All sophomores were *accepted*" means they were *received satisfactorily.*

"All students, *except* sophomores, must report early," means *excluding sophomores.*

You may use *except* as a preposition to mean *outside of*: "No one passed the test *except* Robert." Do not say, "No one passed the test *outside of* Robert."

Accommodate is probably one of the most misspelled words in the English language. Note the double *c* and the double *m.*

Accompanied by. See PARENTHETICAL ELEMENTS.

Active voice. See VOICE.

Actually should not be used to intensify. Not "We *actually* paid seventy-five dollars for it." And not "Betty was *actually* surprised when asked to speak." And certainly not "I *actually* prefer vanilla to chocolate." Drop *actually.* In those examples it adds nothing (not "it *actually* adds nothing") to the meaning of the sentences. But it may be used to express amazement: "Did he *actually* jump off the cliff?"

Definitely is usually just as needless, as in "I *definitely* liked the coat I bought." And saying, "We're *definitely* going to California" doesn't make the going any more definite. Think carefully before using *definitely.* See ADVERBS.

A.D. stands for *anno Domini* and is placed *before* the year: "It was discovered A.D. 320." Do not precede A.D. with "in," since "in" is built into *anno.* Although the *B* in B.C. means "before," B.C. follows the year: "It was first translated in 150 B.C."

Whether to apply A.D. to centuries is a writer's decision. But remember that many regard such usage as inappropriate because a century cannot be in the year of anything.

Speaking of centuries, bear in mind that the twentieth century began on January 1, 1901, and will end on December 31, 2000. Note that the twenty-first century will begin on January 1, 2001, not on January 1, 2000.

Adequate means *enough*, which means that *enough* does not belong in "The number of monitors was *adequate enough* to prevent cheating" and in "The material was *adequate enough* to make such a large awning." A quipster once said, "*Adequate* is enough without enough—enough is enough."

Adjective phrase, a phrase that serves as an adjective, describing or limiting a noun or pronoun. For example, in "The lady at the front door is the proprietor," *at the front door* is an adjective phrase, modifying *lady,* and is introduced by the preposition *at.* Here the phrase follows the noun. In "The defendant *was* in a state of confusion," the phrase *in a state of confusion* follows the linking verb WAS.

Adjectives—the *red* flower, the *tall* boy, a *difficult* task—*modify or limit nouns or pronouns.* But they should not serve as a crutch for a noun that can't stand on its own. As E.B. White says in *The Elements of Style,* "The adjective hasn't been built that can pull a weak or inaccurate noun out of a tight place." This does not disparage the use of adjectives; it is merely a directive to discriminate wisely between their use and misuse, and to consider carefully, before using one, whether it will improve the thought or the description.

Avoid dull and meaningless adjectives (*nice, interesting*) and choose those that are appropriate to the context. This means that you should raise your guard against powerful words that do not belong in ordinary writing (*amazing, fantastic, incredible, unbelievable*) unless an unusually strong reaction is called for, which is seldom.

Admit should not be followed by *to*. Say, "Paul admits his ignorance," not "Paul admits *to* his ignorance."

Adultery is sexual intercourse between a man and a woman when at least one party is married. Otherwise it is *fornication*. Animals *copulate*.

Advance planning. See INNOVATION.

Adverbs modify *verbs, adjectives,* or *other adverbs.* They answer the questions *when, where, how,* and so on: "John plays *well*"; "You must go *now*"; "She threw the ball *farther* than I did."

ADJECTIVES may not properly replace adverbs. Rather than "The supervisor told Jules to do his work as quick as possible," make it "as *quickly* as possible." And in "It's a wonder how helpless a normal, capable man can feel," make it "a *normally* capable man can feel."

Adverbs, like adjectives, are best positioned before the words they modify; otherwise they may affect the meaning, and they will certainly spoil the emphasis. For the sake of accuracy and clarity be particularly careful of *almost, also, even, ever, exactly, just,* and *only.* Rather than "He only gave me five dollars," say "He gave me *only* five dollars," even though the placing of *only* before the verb doesn't mislead anyone. Consider another: "My brother *almost lost* five thousand dollars in the market" becomes "My brother *lost almost* five thousand dollars in the market."

Do not carelessly, and uselessly, introduce a sentence with such adverbs as *obviously, basically,* and *really*: "*Obviously,* vetoing so many bills is foolish" does not indicate what is obvious. It simply indicates an opinion. In "*Basically,* all I want is to marry in July rather than in August," *basically* should be dropped. "I *just* know our trip will be *fantastic*" has two strikes against it. Pitch another and strike it out. *Just* is misused and *fantastic* in this context is a childish word. The best guideline is to mean what you say and to be sure to say only what you mean. Usually the simpler word is more direct and precise.

Affect (verb) means *to influence, to produce a change in,* or *to pretend.* **Effect** (noun) means *result* or *consequence.* Not "Lack of exercise can *effect* one's agility," but "can *affect.*" Nothing can *effect* a person, an institution, or an organization. "The report that said the detour around the center of town seriously *effected* business" is an example of the wrong use of *effect* for *affect.* **Effect** (verb) means *to cause to happen, to bring about*: "The accountant *effected* [verb] changes and their *effect* [noun] was startling." Note that *affect,* as a noun, is a psychological term.

The chances are you will have little use for the

verb *effect* (or the noun *affect*) but will often use its noun form: "The *effect* was. . . ." If a verb is called for, the probabilities are that *affect* is the one you want.

Agenda. See DATA.

Aggravate means *to make worse* or *to intensify*, as "to *aggravate* a wound [or a situation]." But in general usage it means *to annoy* or *to irritate*. In the best English we say, "The extreme cold *aggravated* Grace's bronchitis," but not "My son's disreputable appearance *aggravated* me." Here we would say *vexed*, *exasperated*, or *annoyed*. Again, "A child's misbehavior that irritates or riles a mother may also *aggravate* her illness."

When we use *annoy*, we say we are annoyed *with* a person but *at* a thing or action. If the annoyance comes from an outside source we are annoyed *by*: "First we were annoyed *by* mosquitoes and then *by* gas fumes."

Ago should not be placed alongside *since*. Not "It was only five years *ago since* we bought our house." Change *since* to *that*—"It was only five years ago *that* we bought our house"—or drop *ago* and recast: "It has been only five years *since* we bought our house." See SINCE.

Agree, when used idiomatically, is serviced by several prepositions, each one taking on a different meaning. We say *agree with* of a person, *agree to* of a suggestion, and *agree in* a principle.

Agreement between pronoun and subject. See EACH.

Agreement of subject and verb. See COLLECTIVE NOUNS; SUBJECT OF A SENTENCE; TITLES; NEGATIVE AND POSITIVE SUBJECTS.

Ahold is not a word in the English language. When the sense is *to grasp,* say, for example, "The sailor got *a hold of* [or *grasped* or *grabbed*] the tow line," not got *ahold.*

All followed by *of the* and a noun is in common usage. We say, "All *of the news* is bad" or "All *of the beer* is gone." The *of* is unnecessary, however, and on that account is objected to by some critics. They would prefer "All [no *of*] the news is bad." Nevertheless, whether to omit *of* is simply a matter of taste. Your sense of rhythm and of emphasis must determine. Of course, if *all* is followed by a pronoun, *of* is required: "All *of us* are to attend."

Note that *all,* when used as a pronoun, may be singular or plural, depending on whether an entity or individual items or persons are being considered: "All of the sugar *is* gone," but "All *were* inducted into the army." Note further that in "All I need *is* a shower and a meal," *is* is used correctly. The nouns *shower* and *meal* are PREDICATE NOMINATIVES, while the singular *all* is the subject of the sentence.

Both of is treated in the same manner as *all of.* When followed by a pronoun, *of* is required: "*Both of them* agreed to come." Otherwise *of* is optional. Use *of* if you think it makes the sentence read more smoothly. "Both men [or *both of the men*] agreed to come." See INDEFINITE PRONOUNS.

All-around is not the way to describe a person whose abilities or talents you consider the best. The proper word is *all-round*. *All-around* refers to a position with a center as the focal point. The sense of *all-round* is full or complete.

All intents and purposes is a very old phrase that has seen so much semantic service that it is now considered trite. A writer should think of something fresher. Furthermore, the phrase is often used meaninglessly. When that is so, it surely should be dropped. In "The president of our company *to all intents and purposes* is the one who makes the final decisions," the key phrase serves no useful purpose.

Alliteration, a succession of similar sounds, as in "Peter Piper picked a peck of pickled peppers," is generally condemned as an affectation, but it can be used effectively if discretion is exercised. It certainly was a telling device in Thomas Paine's famous declaration: "These are the times that try men's souls." But writers should carefully consider both need and advisability before using this rhetorical device.

All ready. See ALTOGETHER.

All right is often seen spelled, in informal writing, as *alright*. As one wit remarked, "*Alright* is okay for those who write *alwrong*." See ANY TIME.

All together. See ALTOGETHER.

Allude/refer point to something; *allude*, indirectly—that is, without mentioning it explicitly

("He *alluded* to Shakespeare when he spoke about the Bard of Avon")—*refer*, directly ("The teacher *referred* to *Macbeth* as being an outstanding piece of poetry.") Someone or something identified is *referred to*, not *alluded to*.

Be sure to distinguish between *elude*, which means *to escape* or *to avoid someone or something*, and *allude*. The similar sounds of these words may cause confusion. Do not say, "The speaker *eluded* to the cold winter when he shuddered and rubbed his hands together." He *alluded*.

Almost. See ADVERBS.

Already. See ALTOGETHER.

Also ordinarily should not begin a sentence. Use *in addition* or *furthermore* or an equivalent, or shift its position in the sentence. Instead of "*Also* they will serve their country," say, "They *also* will serve their country." But note how important the placement of *also* can be: "They will *also* serve their country" has a different connotation from "They *also* will serve their country." The former means *in addition to what they are doing*. The latter means *they as well as other people*.

Inverted sentences may properly begin with *also* ("*Also* in the loss column were the pharmaceuticals"), but this usage is a rarity. See ADVERBS.

Alternate (adjective) means *following in turns, first one and then the other* (on *alternate* Mondays). The established meaning of its noun form is *substitute* ("an *alternate* delegate"). An **alternative** (noun), strictly speaking, is a choice between two possibilities. However, that restriction no longer holds. *Alternative* is widely used of any number: "The *alternatives* are to fight, to surrender, or to commit suicide"; Four *alternative* economic plans were suggested." Of course, using *choice* where three or more options are involved is still a good choice.

Alternative. See ALTERNATE.

Although/though are interchangeable in most contexts. The choice is up to you, and depends only upon which sentence rhythm you find preferable: "We decided to go, *although/though* we knew the trip would be arduous."

Although is somewhat more formal than *though*, but *though* is more versatile. It can follow *even* ("I hope, *even though* I know it will never be"); *although* cannot. Furthermore *though* may end a sentence ("He agreed, *though*"); *although* should not.

Altogether means *entirely, thoroughly, completely*: "She might as well ignore it *altogether*." **All together** (two words) means *at the same time* or *in one place*. Its sense is *grouped*: "The legislators were *all together* in the rotunda." Notice that *all* in *all together* is unnecessary to the sense of the sentence, since *all together* means "together": "The legislators were *together* in the rotunda." But the *all* may be used if it is thought to add emphasis.

This thinking (the addition of *all*) applies as well to *all ready* (meaning *prepared*) but not to *already* (meaning *earlier* or *previously*). "We are *all ready* to leave" needs no *all*. *Already*, on the other hand, an adverb of time, of course needs its *al-*.

A.M./P.M. are abbreviations of time, A.M. referring to the hours between midnight and noon; P.M., to the hours between noon and midnight. The abbreviation for noon is M., but it is safer to use *noon*.

Avoid such phrases as "9:30 A.M. in the morning" and "3:30 P.M. in the afternoon." Choose either A.M. or *in the morning*, but do not use both A.M. and *in the morning*; likewise, not both P.M. and *in the afternoon*.

Words are used with *o'clock*: "six o'clock."

Amazing. See ADJECTIVES.

Ambiguous/equivocal both refer to statements that are susceptible to two or more interpretations. The difference between these words in application is that what is *ambiguous* usually comes from carelessness, whereas what is *equivocal* is intentional. An *ambiguous* statement, it may be said, is made by a person who has failed to make himself clear; an *equivocal* statement is made by someone who is purposely deceptive.

Among. See BETWEEN.

Amount refers to an *aggregate*, to *quantities viewed in bulk, things involving a unified mass*: "This large *amount* of lumber must have cost a large *amount* of money," and figuratively, "We'll need a large *amount* of time, patience, and humor to finish this job." Most nouns following *amount* are singular. **Number** is used of *countable things*; that is, things that can be counted in individual units: "The *number* of the books on the shelf does not exceed twenty-five." *Number* is normally used with plural nouns.

Ampersand, symbolized by &, should be used only in the names of firms or groups that use it themselves, or in abridged matter. Otherwise write *and*.

An. See A.

And joins dual subjects (similar elements by way of addition), which generally take plural verbs ("The peaches and the bananas *are* not ripe"), but singular verbs if the subjects are thought of as a unit and therefore have a meaning essentially singular ("Ham and cheese *is* my favorite sandwich"; "The wear and tear *was* more than expected").

It is best not to use *and* in place of *to* before an infinitive, as in "Be sure *and* come" or in "Try *and* do it neatly." Say, "Be sure *to* come" and "Try *to* do it neatly."

And can anyone think of a good reason why a sentence should not begin with *and* (or *but*)? Of course not. In fact, it is a good device to draw attention to what follows. But use it sparingly. See AMPERSAND; AND/OR; AND WHICH; CONJUNCTIONS; SINGULAR AND PLURAL NOUNS; SUBJECT OF A SENTENCE.

And/or is used primarily in legal or business communications. It means that there are three choices involving two elements. "The judge may impose a fine *and*/or a prison term" means that the defendant may be fined or imprisoned or subjected to both a fine and imprisonment.

In general, this device is best avoided, certainly in formal writing. Not everyone can grasp its meaning easily, and some object to its unsightly appearance. Rather than "You may have succotash *and*/

or zucchini," make it, "You may have succotash *or* zucchini *or* both."

And others. See INCLUDE/INCLUDING.

And which (and **but which**) presupposes a preceding *which*, which means that the pronoun *which* must appear at least once by itself: "The project, *which* we know so well, *and which* the papers excoriated, is about to begin." **And who** is governed by the same restrictions. Do not say, "Stout women of middle age and who do light work should watch their diet." Omit *and*. But we do say, "Men *who* do strenuous work, *and who* take care of household chores, may be suffering from great tension." Or, "This is the girl *whom* I love *and whom* I intend to marry."

Annoy. See AGGRAVATE.

Another. See INDEFINITE PRONOUNS.

Antecedent—the grammatical term for the word to which a pronoun refers. Since the pronoun stands for the noun (the *antecedent*), the pronoun must agree with the noun in PERSON, NUMBER, and GENDER. In "When we found the horses, they were bathed in perspiration," *horses* is the antecedent of *they*. Both the antecedent and the pronoun are third person, plural, and neuter.

An antecedent should be unmistakably referred to by a following pronoun. This is not so in "Notwithstanding the stenographer's fatigue, *it* was typed perfectly." In fact *it* referring to a document has no antecedent. In "Sherwood told Paul that he was about to travel," you might ask to whom does *he* refer? It would be better to reword: "*I* am about to travel," Sherwood told Paul, or "Paul, *you* are about to travel," Sherwood said, as the case might be.

An antecedent does not belong inside a SUBORDINATE CLAUSE. Place it in the main clause. Change "The bird, whose *feathers* were matted down by the rain, shook *them* free and flew away" to "The bird freed its feathers, which had been matted down by rain, and then flew away." And note that a noun in the possessive case may not serve as an antecedent for a pronoun. In "Bob's father says he doesn't believe he will attend," the antecedent is confusing. Who is not going to attend—Bob or his father? Make it, "Bob's father says he doesn't believe Bob will attend" or some other clear phrasing.

One thing more: Although a pronoun seldom precedes its antecedent, in rare cases it may. For instance, "In all *his* life, *Clyde* had never witnessed a murder." *Clyde* is the antecedent of *his*. See PRONOUNS.

Anticipate, although considered a synonym of **expect**, should not be used where *expect* is called for. To anticipate is *to foresee* and *to act against*: "The lawyer's presentation showed that he had *anticipated* the arguments of his adversary." To *expect* is to look forward to: "I *expect* to have a young woman visit me today."

Do not use *anticipate* in the passive voice (not "The economic decline *was anticipated*") or follow it with an infinitive (not "The decline was anticipated *to occur*"), but you may say ". . . was *expected* to occur." Those restrictions are not imposed on *expect*.

Anticipatory subject. See IT.

Anxious, in general usage, is a replacement for **eager**: "I'm *anxious* to get tickets for the Super Bowl." In better discourse *anxious* is used only when it implies desire mixed with uncertainty or worry. An *anxious* person is ill at ease or distressed in mind. A guest may tell her host that she is "*anxious* to leave for home before the snow starts." *Eager* is the word to use to imply enthusiasm and impatience.

Any. See INDEFINITE PRONOUN.

Any and all. See CANNOT AND WILL NOT.

Anymore, an adverb of time, meaning *not now, though formerly*, should appear at the end of a thought and be used negatively; that is, with a negative word: "We don't do that *anymore*"; "He doesn't swim *anymore*" or with a question: "Does Doris live in Phoenix *anymore*?"; "Will he be away *anymore*?"

Whether to spell the expression as two words or as one solid word is a writer's choice. In current use the one-word styling is more common: "I don't visit him *anymore*." Although some spelling mavens recommend that *anymore* should be written solid in all cases, more discriminating grammarians say that the phrase *any more* where *more* is used as a pronoun or adjective must be written as just noted, as two words: "The pillows are very pretty, but we don't need *any more*."

Anyone refers to persons in general. It is a solid word and the stress is on *any*: "*Anyone* who is interested may attend." **Any one** refers to one person or thing in a specific group. The stress in these two words is on *one*: "*Any one* of those neckties will do."

When not sure which of these terms is called for, see whether *anybody* can be substituted. If so, *anyone* is required. In other cases *any one* is the correct form.

Anyplace (everyplace, someplace)—the "place" adverb, usually spelled as one word—is an undesirable substitute for *anywhere* (*everywhere, somewhere*), despite the protestations of Webster. "We did not see it *anywhere*" is preferable to "We did not see it *anyplace*." But we do say, "We did not see it in *any* [adjective] *place* [noun] we looked."

Attaching an *s* to *anywhere*, to pluralize it (*anywheres*), is to create a nonexistent form. Even though we may have looked in many places, we do not say, at least not correctly, "We could not find it *anywheres*."

Which brings up the question of *noplace*. It is not in standard usage, any more than *nowheres*.

Any time should be spelled as given, with two words. And so should **all right.** It should be noted, however, that some authorities (Webster, Flesch) prefer the one word *anytime*, a consolidation that agrees with other "any" words: *anyway, anything, anymore,* and so on. See ALL RIGHT.

Anywhere. See ANYPLACE.

Anywheres. See ANYPLACE.

Apparent refers to that which, according to the senses, appears to exist. Nevertheless, although appearing as such, it may not necessarily be so ("an *apparent* thief"). That which is **evident** has been established by some objective proof, by some external sign or signs. It is unmistakable. Therefore, rather than "Ralph *evidently* is lying," if what is meant is that he seems to be lying, prefer "Ralph is *apparently lying.*"

Unfortunately, two contradictory meanings have evolved for *apparent: obvious* and *seeming.* Dictionaries offer these irreconcilable senses without explanations. The wisest approach, therefore, is to use *seeming* if you mean seeming, and *obvious* if you mean obvious. If one were to say, "It is apparent that Walt is going," it could mean "*obviously* Walt is going" or "*it seems that* Walt is going." Be careful.

Appoint. See CONSIDER.

Appositive—a word or phrase placed near another word to identify or explain it. For example, in "Murphy, *our accountant,* will be here soon," *our accountant* explains who Murphy is. In "San Diego, *a city in Southern California,* is famous for its zoo," *a city in Southern California* tells us what San Diego is. And in "My cousin *Edwin* was elected," *Edwin* identifies the cousin. Note that in the first two examples the information in the appositive is not essential and that it is therefore set off by commas. But in the third example no commas set off the appositive, because what has been added—*Edwin*—is essential.

Caveat: The appositive must be in the same case

as the lead word. Not "The officers, Jim and me, will go to the convention," but "Jim and *I*." The subject *officers* is in the nominative case, hence the nominative form of the pronoun—*I*. Not "The dancers, Stella and her, will take the leading roles," but "Stella and *she*." And not "*Let's* you and I do it," because *let's* stands for *let us*. Make it *you and me*, since the lead word *us* is in the objective case. Thus, correctly put, is objective case-objective case; that is, the *us* in *let's* and the *me* in *you and me*. See PARENTHETICAL ELEMENTS.

Appraise means *to evaluate*, usually *to set a monetary value*. **Apprise** means *to inform*. "Burton will *appraise* your jewelry and *apprise* you of the results sometime tomorrow."

Appreciate means *to recognize the quality, significance, or magnitude of*. But in everyday conversation *appreciate* is often used as a replacement for *understand*: "I *appreciate* your request; however, our store is now closed." Be careful not to limit the scope of *appreciate*. It has come to mean *realize*. In certain contexts *realize* and *understand* are synonymous.

In business, *appreciate* means *to increase in value*: "Because of the rise in the stock market, many individuals have securities that have *appreciated* considerably."

Apt. See LIABLE/LIKELY/APT.

Arithmetical phrases. See PLUS.

Around. See ABOUT.

Articles—*a, an, the*—are not listed as one of the PARTS OF SPEECH because technically they are adjectives. Both *a* and *an* are indefinite articles, since they point to nothing specific ("I have *a* history book"). *The* indicates something particular ("*The* red book is a history book").

As needs careful attention both to avoid undesirable colloquialisms and to achieve precision. The expressions *as good as* ("He *as good as* admitted it") and *as much as* ("He *as much as* admitted it") do not belong in better writing. In either case prefer *practically*, and for *as much* (without the second *as*) use the pronoun *this*: "He admitted *this* [not *as much*] to his lawyer."

In a sentence such as "Gert has lived here as long as *I/me*," the correct choice is *I*. The omitted words would clarify: "Gert has lived here as long as I *have lived here*." In "Al Janover speaks Spanish as fluently as *I/me*," here again the omitted word would supply the correct choice: "as fluently as I *do*." See BECAUSE; LIKE; THAN; OMISSION OF WORDS.

As . . . as/so . . . as are used to make comparisons. *As . . . as* is used in either positive or negative statements, but *so . . . as* is preferred by careful writers when making negative comparisons: "Although John is almost *as* tall *as* Bob, Albert is not *so* tall *as* either one." See THAN.

As if/as though are interchangeable. But be sure not to substitute *like* for either one. Not "This chicken tastes *like* it was dragged through the mud," but *as if* or *as though*. And not "It looks *like* it's going to rain." Here again, choose either *as if* or *as though*. See LIKE.

Whether to use *was* or *were* after these forms—it looks *as if* or *as though* it *was* or *were* (*were* is the subjunctive form)—depends on the level of writing. In formal contexts *were* is expected. In informal contexts *was* is often seen, although *were* would be preferable even there.

As much. See AS.

Assemble/cooperate/mix—all have a sense of togetherness. Hence do not accompany any of these words with *together*.

As though. See AS IF/AS THOUGH.

As to, except when it is used at the beginning of a sentence to introduce an element otherwise postponed ("*As to* Fred, we think he will serve the board well"), is best replaced by a single preposition: "The established rules *as to* [*of*] conduct were ignored." "There was no doubt *as to* [*about*] the nature of the contract."

Avoid the combination *as to whether*. In "He raised the question *as to whether* Mark is competent," *as to* should be omitted. Remember that the word *question* is never properly followed by *as to whether* but by *whether* alone.

As well as may be a source of ambiguity in some sentences. "Lester plays the harmonica *as well as* Sylvia" may mean either that Lester's playing is *as good as* Sylvia's or simply that *he too* plays the harmonica. Change to reflect the intended sense:

"Lester and Sylvia play the harmonica *equally well*" or "*Both* Lester and Sylvia play the harmonica." Note that *both* is never a suitable companion for *as well as*. Therefore, not "We spotted *both* Libbie *as well as* her sister on the boardwalk." Omit *both*, or change *as well as* to *and*.

When *as well as* comes between the subject and the verb, the phrase has no bearing on the number of the verb. This means that if the subject is singular, the verb must be singular: "The *architect*, as well as his three assistants, *is* due shortly." Note that the sentence is clearer when the *as well as* phrase is set off by commas. See BOTH; PARENTHETICAL ELEMENTS.

At does not belong after *where*. Not "*Where* is the elevator *at*?" or "*Where* do you live *at*?" Omit *at*. It is as superfluous as *to* in "*Where* did he go *to*?" See ABOUT; PREPOSITIONS.

At about. See ABOUT.

Attributive adjective. See SIMILAR.

Audience. See COLLECTIVE NOUNS.

Author, in the opinion of many authorities, is a noun and not a verb. These authorities would criticize this sentence—"John T. Simmons authored a book on jogging"—and would revise it to read: "John T. Simmons is the author of a book on jogging." But remember that some reputable writers do use *author* as a verb—a usage, nevertheless, that is not recommended here.

Avenge/revenge have different senses, yet the distinction between them is not always clear. The verb *avenge* represents a higher motive than the verb *revenge*. *To avenge* is *to mete out punishment for a wrong inflicted on another person.* It might be said that the avenger is seeking to redress an injustice. *To revenge* is *to seek retaliation for a wrong done to the revenger.* It is an action taken for personal satisfaction or gratification.

Aware. See CONSCIOUS.

Awful. See VERY.

Awhile is an adverb: "I'll rest *awhile.*" If you wish to use a preposition (*for* or *in*) for the sake of rhythm or emphasis, you must use the noun *while*: "I'll rest *for a while*; I'll see you *in a while.*" Be aware that the same idea is expressed in "Stay *awhile*" and in "Stay *for a while.*"

B

Back of/in back of are regarded as colloquial or informal phrases. In better writing use *behind*: "The playing field is *behind* [not *in back of*] the gymnasium." However, "in *the* back of" is considered standard English.

The sister term *in front of*, unlike *in back of*, has been accepted on the highest level of the language. True, *before*, a synonym, is economical, but it can't always replace *in front of*. For example, "*In front of* our house stands a large maple tree" reads smoothly. "*Before* our house stands a large maple tree" sounds clumsy.

Backward/backwards. See TOWARD/TOWARDS.

Bad/badly need special attention, since they are so frequently used, and misused. *Bad* is an adjective and should, after a LINKING VERB, modify the subject. This occurs when it follows a form of *to be* or verbs of the senses such as *look, taste, smell,* and *touch*: "Ray looks *bad*"; "Doug feels *bad*." *Badly* is an adverb and serves active verbs: "Old man Thompson has lost his sense of touch; he feels *badly*." Although "I feel *badly*," meaning *not well*, is commonly used in speech, be on guard against it, especially in writing.

One thing more: "Thomas wants a part in the

play *badly"* could just as well be framed using *very much*. Certainly in better writing it should be.

Balance is a word that has so many useful meanings that it needn't be given another, especially one that is unsuitable—a reference to time. When speaking of that part of the day that is still left, do not use *balance*: "the *balance* of the day." Use *rest* or *remainder* instead: "We will spend the *rest* [or the *remainder*] of the week at Aunt Harriet's house."

Barely/hardly/scarcely have negative qualities, since their sense is "almost not" or "probably not." Therefore, to avoid the effect of a double negative, they should not be used with another negative in the same sentence. Not "We have scarcely no sugar left," but "We have *scarcely any* sugar left." Not "We can't barely see the shoreline," but "We *can barely* see the shoreline." In "He saved hardly nothing," a change to *anything* is needed. And since these adverbs are not comparatives, complete them with *when*, not *than*. Not "We had hardly opened the door than we heard the telephone ring," but "We had *hardly* opened the door *when* we heard the telephone ring."

The expression *can't hardly* ("I *can't hardly* wait for my son's homecoming") is incorrectly used for *can hardly*. *Hardly* means "probably not." See THAN.

Basically. See ADVERBS.

B.C. See A.D.

Because should not be used in the same related sequence with *the reason is*, for they mean the same thing, which makes *the reason is because* redundant. Not "The reason I left at three o'clock was because I had another appointment," but "*The reason* I left at three o'clock was *that* I had another appointment" or "I left at three o'clock *because* I had another appointment." Or use *since,* a shorter but less formal word.

Because, as, since, and *for* may introduce words that give the reason. *Because* is the most emphatic. *As* may lead to ambiguity. Be careful. "*As* he was leaving, she yelled at him" may mean "*because* he was leaving" or "*while* he was leaving." *Since* is a good crisp word. *For* is the most formal. See AS; BEING AS/BEING THAT/BEING AS HOW; SINCE.

Begging the question does not mean being evasive by talking around the subject or by ignoring it. The expression means that one assumes as true the point of the discussion, the truth of which is the issue. Or, as defined by Webster, "to employ an argument that assumes as valid the very same argument that one is trying to prove."

A common example of begging the question occurs in a discussion of whether there is a God. If one party said, "Of course there is a God, because He controls the universe," that person would be *begging the question.*

Begin has many synonyms, but all are best used in different contexts. For example, *commence, inaugurate,* and *initiate* have the sense of *a beginning,* but those words should be confined to the description of formal or ceremonious occasions. They certainly are too heavy for ordinary use. *Start* is closer in sense to *begin* and, in fact, the words are often interchangeable. But here again, there are shades of difference that give each word its own semantic niche. *Start* implies a quicker, perhaps a more unexpected, beginning than *begin*. We *start* a race or a motor, but we *begin* a letter. We *begin* a meal—and we *begin* to look old.

Behalf, if preceded by *on* (*on behalf of*), means *on the part of* or *acting as the agent of*. A lawyer goes to court *on behalf of* his client. If *behalf* is preceded by *in* (*in behalf of*), its sense is *in support of* or *for the benefit of*: "The Police Athletic League was established *in behalf of* fatherless boys."

Being as/being that/being as how should not replace *since* or *because* or *inasmuch as* or *owing to the fact that*. Not "*Being that* [or *being as how*] I have no piano lesson today, I'm going to play tennis," but "*Because* [or *since*] I have no piano lesson today, I'm going to play tennis."

    Seeing as how is likewise undesirable. Do not say or write, "*Seeing as how* it's raining so hard, I'll stay indoors all day." Use one of the replacement terms provided above.

Beside. See BESIDES.

Besides means *in addition to*. A quipster might say that in addition to being misused, it is sometimes even misspelled. The source of this trouble is its look-alike *beside*, which means *alongside* or *next to*. Hence "A movie star sat besides me" needs *beside*, and "*Beside* his loss of hearing, the patient also suffered from double vision" needs *besides*. It's easy to confuse this pair.

Be sure and. See AND.

Between implies *two*. Not "He stuttered between each word," but *between every two words* or *between words*. And not "We had a drink between each inning," but *between innings*. Always follow *between* with a plural noun. **Among** suggests that three or more persons or things are involved: "He divided the money *among* the three children." But if the relationship is one of several individual things considered as pairs, *between* is rightly used of any number: "A pact was reached *between* the four European nations"; "The campus is situated *between* Allen, Rathbone, and Poplar streets."

Between is invariably followed by *and* when a choice is indicated. Not "Paul must choose between Sally or me," but "*between* Sally *and* me." Not "It must be between forty to fifty degrees," but "*between* forty *and* fifty degrees."

Caveat: Do not follow *between* with a *-self* pronoun. Not "It was a secret between Irving and myself," but "*between* Irving and *me*." Prepositions, of which *between* is one, take pronouns in the objective case. Hence *between you and me*. One who says "just *between you and I*" marks himself as being only partly educated. See REFLEXIVE PRONOUNS.

Bi- prefixes cause confusion in the words **bimonthly** and **biweekly** because dictionaries give two irreconcilable meanings: "every two . . ." and "twice a . . ." Certainly the best way to avoid misunderstanding is to spell out what is meant: *every two weeks, twice a week, every other week*. Other *bi-* words are clear in any context: **biannual** means *twice a year* and **biennial** means *every two years*.

Since many experts hold that *bimonthly* means *every two months* (*bi* meaning *every two*) and that *semimonthly* means *twice a month* (*semi* meaning *half*), it is a writer's decision whether to apply these terms to represent these meanings.

Blame should be followed by *for*, not *on*. Not "They blamed the accident *on* me," but "They *blamed* me *for* the accident," which places the blame where it belongs. Do not attribute blame to inanimate objects. For example, do not say, "I blame that dumb elevator for tearing my dress," since the elevator cannot feel or accept blame. **Caveat:** The conventional hold of this idiom is loosening. Some experts today say that you may blame something on someone: "The coach *blamed* the *loss* on *himself*." In formal writing, nevertheless, stay with tradition: *blame for*.

Blonde (noun) is used of a woman: "She is a *blonde*." **Blond** (noun) is used of a man. Either form may be used as an adjective and applied to either sex, but prefer *blond* (with no *e*): "Her *blond* hair."

Both means *two considered together*. **Each** means *one of two or more*. We say "*both* of the children made outstanding grades" and "*each* is to receive a scholarship." But not, for example, "both children wore a new hat." Correctly, "*each* child wore a new hat," unless the one hat was so large that the two children could get under it at the same time.

When things are considered separately, use *each*, not *both*. If one were to say, "We were both given an apple," a question might arise whether there were two apples or one to be shared.

Caution: Both lends itself to many redundancies. Avoid "They were *both alike*"; "They are *both equally* good"; "The books were *both identical.*" Omit *both* in each instance.

Since *both* is used in reference only to two persons or things, do not say, "Adrienne is both pretty, charming, and intelligent." Drop *both*. *Both* used as a conjunction invariably takes *and*. Hence "She is both pretty as well as charming" is wrongly put. Insert *and* for *as well as* or omit *both*. See AS WELL AS; INDEFINITE PRONOUNS.

Both . . . and. See CORRELATIVE CONJUNCTIONS.

Both of. See ALL.

Brand. See CONSIDER.

Bring/take indicate opposite directions. *Bring* implies motion toward the speaker; *take,* away from the speaker. The sense of *bring* is to *come with* something; *take,* to *go with* something. "*Take* this note to your teacher and *bring* me her reply."

Idiom pays no attention to such precise meanings. We say, for example, "I'll be *taking* home my pay," but "I'll be *bringing* home the bacon."

Burglar. See ROBBER/THIEF/BURGLAR.

But, in its most common use, is a conjunction ("We would like to go, *but* it's too warm"), yet it can also be a preposition (meaning *except*) or an adverb (the equivalent of *only*). Its use as an adverb is for-

mal: "In the library there was *but* one reference
librarian." Remember that, when used as a preposition, *but* takes nouns and pronouns in the objective
(not the nominative) case. Not "Everyone attended
but Kevin and I," but "Kevin and *me.*" Note that
no comma preceded the *but.*

But is not a suitable escort for *nevertheless* or
yet. Do not say, "*But nevertheless* we'll go" or "*But
yet* it will come to pass." Omit the *but.* See AND;
CONJUNCTIONS.

But what is not approved for better writing. Not
"Bertram doesn't know but what he should leave
early," but "*whether* he should leave early," and
not "We are not sure but what the plane has already taken off," but "We are not sure *that* the
plane has already taken off."

A sentence with the word *help,* meaning *refrain
from,* needs no *but* or *but what.* In "We can't help
but wonder," omit *but* and change *wonder* to *wondering* (a GERUND): "We can't *help wondering.*"
According to some writers, the phrase *can't help
but* is idiomatically established. Nevertheless, it is
a clumsy combination and should be avoided. A
sister expression, as in "Don't miss more sessions
than you *can help,*" is properly given as "Don't
miss more sessions than you *must.*"

But which. See AND WHICH.

C

Called. See HYPHENS.

Can suggests mental or physical ability: "He *can* [that is, he is *able to*] swim the channel." "What is possible *can* be done." In everyday speech, however, the word of ability, *can*, is displacing the word of permission, *may*: "You *can* go when I dismiss the class, but no sooner."

The colloquial commingling of *can* and *may* could lead to ambiguity. Consider the sentence "He *can* walk to the theater." In formal English this means he is able to do so. Colloquially, it means either he has permission to do so or he is capable of navigating that distance on foot. Which, to say the least, is less than precise. See MAY/MIGHT; MIXED TENSES.

Cannot and will not is a redundant and trite expression. Avoid it. Use the one element that is more appropriate—either *cannot* or *will not*. Treat "any and all," "unless and until," and "if and when" in the same way.

Can't hardly. See BARELY.

Can't help but. See BUT WHAT.

Carat/caret/karat are pronounced alike but have

33

different meanings. *Carat* (with two *a*'s) is a unit of weight for gems. *Caret* is a mark by an editor (notice the *e*'s in both *caret* and *editor*) to indicate an insertion (^). *Karat* (again with two *a*'s) is a unit of fineness of gold.

Cardinal numbers. See FIRST, SECOND, THIRD.

Caret. See CARAT.

Cause was due to is a redundancy. Not "The cause of the delay was due to an early accident on the road." Either omit *cause of*, leaving "The delay was due to an early accident," or omit *due to*, making it "The cause of the delay was an early accident on the road."

Cement holds together the concrete used in walkways. Although we speak of *a cement sidewalk*, be aware that it is really a *concrete* sidewalk, cement being just one ingredient in concrete.

Center around is an expression accepted by many formal stylists but deplored by others. Instead of "The play *centered around* a Machiavellian character," they would use *on* or *upon* for *around* or change *centered* to *revolved* (*revolved around*). Although strictly speaking the expression is illogical, for something cannot be centered *around*, it nevertheless is regarded as good idiom.

Centuries. See A.D.

Character is what you are. **Reputation** is what people think you are. To put it in another way—*char-*

acter is a person's *actual* nature; *reputation*, her or his *supposed* nature.

Claim (verb) should be used to mean *to demand as a matter of right or title*. It should not replace such words as *assert*, *declare*, *maintain*, *profess*, *protest*, *remark*, and the ordinary *say*. You may say, properly, "He *claims* to be the owner of the hotel," but not "He *claims* his city is the best place to live."

Class. See COLLECTIVE NOUNS.

Clause—*a group of related words that contains a subject and a predicate*. The sentence "My cousin's racing car, which he bought last year, won the last race," contains two clauses. The one that can stand by itself is variously called a *main, chief, independent,* or *principal* clause. In this example it is *My cousin's racing car won the last race.* The one that cannot stand alone is called a *dependent* clause. In the example it is *which he bought last year.* See SUBORDINATE CLAUSE.

Clauses of comparison. See ELLIPSIS.

Cleave. See SCAN.

Clothes. See SINGULAR AND PLURAL NOUNS.

Cohort is not a synonym of *associate* or *companion*. An individual is never a *cohort*, which originally was a division of the Roman army. Its current meaning is *company* or *band*, as in "The Republican chairman has gotten his *cohort* of rooters ready for the acceptance speech."

Collective ideas. See AND.

Collective nouns, those that describe a group of people or things—*apparatus, audience, committee, company, flock, majority, public, team,* and so on—although expressed in singular form may be treated as either singular or plural, depending on the collective involved. Some collective nouns are always treated as singulars: *apparatus, news, summons.* Others—*assets, means, premises, savings, wages*—are always plural. Still others are treated as singular or plural according to the meaning intended.

If regarded as a unit, a collective noun takes a singular verb: "That fat *couple was* the first to pay"; "The *jury is* leaving the jury room"; The *class is* large." If the members are considered individually, the plural sense requires a plural verb: "The *jury are* disagreeing among themselves"; "My *family are* all ill." If a collective noun with a plural sense sounds awkward, use *members of, officials of,* and so on ("The *members of* the jury *are* disagreeing among themselves").

Do not treat a collective noun as both a singular and a plural in the same sentence. Maintain a consistent agreement between verb and pronoun. Not "Sears *is* closing *their* local branch," but "*its* local branch." Not "True community spirit will not exist until the citizenry *acts* as one for the welfare of *their* community," but "for the welfare of *its* community." See COUPLE; EACH; FRACTIONS; SINGULAR AND PLURAL NOUNS; WEIGHTS, MONEY, MEASUREMENTS.

Combine into one is a redundant expression. If something is combined, two or more objects have been made into one. Omit *into one*.

Commence. See BEGIN.

Committee. See COLLECTIVE NOUNS.

Common. See MUTUAL.

Company. See COLLECTIVE NOUNS.

Comparative forms of adjectives compare two persons or things: "He is *better* than you"; "This pillow is *larger* than that one"; "Today is *pleasanter* than yesterday." When you compare a person or thing with other members of the same class, exclude the first item from the class by using *other* or *else*. But this was not done in "Chicago is larger than any city in Illinois." According to that statement, Chicago is larger than Chicago, since it is a city in Illinois. And that, of course, is nonsense. Add *other* to *any* ("any *other* city in Illinois"). If you say, "Rachel is a better dancer than anyone on the Pennbrook dancing team," you're saying that Rachel is not a member of the dancing team. But if you say, "Rachel is a better dancer than anyone *else* on the Pennbrook dancing team," we know that Rachel is a member of the team.

In "He made no *other* drawing but that one," *but* should be changed to *than*. After comparatives and *else*, *other*, and *otherwise*, *than* is required.

A further thought: In everyday speech a superlative sometimes replaces a comparative form, even though a comparative is technically required: "Put your best foot forward"; "Between Arthur and Halley, who do you think is the best candidate?"; "We traveled to Paris and Rome. I liked Paris the best." See ELLIPSIS; OMISSION OF WORDS; SUPERLATIVE FORMS; THAN.

Comparative subjects. See AND.

Compared. See AS.

Compare with/compare to are both acceptable idioms, but each is used differently. The former serves when an actual comparison of things or persons of the same kind is being made to discover their likenesses and their differences. The *with* comparison is usually a real one rather than one that is metaphorical: "Let's compare Emerson's opinions *with* those of Carlyle"; "The auditor would like to compare this year's figures *with* last year's." The comparison with *to* stresses similarities, although what is being compared on the whole is rather dissimilar than similar, its sense being figurative. "Our teacher compared a light bulb *to* the sun"; "Our muscle-bound coach is often compared *to* an oak tree"; "The beautician compared the model's skin *to* ivory."

Comparisons, if not properly structured, may be ambiguous. For example, "Estelle's cooking is far better than her mother" is comparing *cooking* with Estelle's *mother.* Correct by saying, "far better than her *mother's* cooking" or "Estelle's cooking is better than *that* of her mother."

In some comparisons of equality, *as* is often overlooked. Not "Rachel sings as well and, in some songs, better than Stella," but "Rachel sings as well *as* and, in some songs, better than Stella." Don't forget the second *as.*

When using the word *compared*, be sure that the items it links are comparable. In "My grades *compared* with Robin were low," a change is required to "*those* of Robin" or "with *Robin's.*" See ELLIPSIS; COMPARATIVE FORMS; UNIQUE.

Compile. See COMPOSE/COMPILE.

Complacent/complaisant are two words that cause writers to run to a speller before using them. And no one has come up with a mnemonic device to help those distraught writers. The shorter word, *complacent*, means *smug* or *being pleased with oneself*. The longer and pleasanter word, *complaisant*, means *eager to please others*. The longer word is fast disappearing in favor of the shorter one, which more and more is coming to represent both meanings. Nevertheless, it is wise for a concerned writer to stay with tradition by spelling and using these words correctly.

Complected is not a word in the English language. A person of dark skin is "dark-*complexioned*," not "dark-*complected*," despite Webster's listing of *dark-complected* as standard English.

Complement means *to fill out, to make whole*. It suggests the addition of something necessary to complete. It is both a noun—"We now have our full *complement* of violinists"—and a verb—"The earrings *complemented* her coiffure."

A **compliment** is approval or praise. What is surprising is the number of times one sees these words misused for one another. Be careful. Distinguish the spelling of these words by remembering that *complement* means to complete and that *complement* has two *e*'s, just as *complete* has.

In grammar, a *complement* is a word or a group

of words used to complete the meaning of a verb: "Tom is an *engineer*" (predicate nominative); "The children are *hungry*" (predicate adjective); "We saw the *Getsons*" (direct object); "Lydia gave *Maurice* [indirect object] the dictionary"; "The team elected Tom *captain*" (objective complement).

Compose/compile generally are used in different contexts. *To compose is to arrange into a single finished work*—a poem, a sonata, a document. *To compile is to acquire and put in order all material that forms a book or other literary product.* In some cases the meanings of the words overlap, but a book, like this one, is said to have been compiled.

Composed of. See COMPRISE.

Comprise means *to consist of* or *to be composed of.* The whole comprises the parts. The parts do not comprise the whole; they *constitute* or *make up* the whole. Therefore, not "Three trucks and sixteen men *comprise* our fire-fighting unit," but "Our fire-fighting unit *comprises* three trucks and sixteen men." "The apartment *comprises* two bedrooms, a living room, a kitchen, and a bathroom." "The encyclopedia *comprises* fourteen volumes."

Note that *comprise* is used only in the active voice, never in the passive (not *is comprised of*). We may say, however, "Our fire-fighting unit *is composed of* three trucks and sixteen men" or switch to another word in the active voice: *consists.* See INCLUDE/INCLUDING.

Conjunctions are *words used to join words or a group of words, such as a phrase or a clause.* Common conjunctions are *and, but, or,* and *nor*: "He is tall *and* handsome"; "Tom *or* Bill will deliver the package." See AND; BUT; CONJUNCTIVE ADVERBS; CORRELATIVE CONJUNCTIONS; OR; NOR; SUBORDINATING CONJUNCTIONS.

Conjunctive adverbs (*accordingly, also, besides, consequently, furthermore, hence, however, likewise, moreover, nevertheless, otherwise, still, then, therefore,* etc.) are words of transition. That is, they tell the reader how a thought that preceded or a thought to follow is related to the rest of the sentence. To put it differently, they serve as logical connectors of thoughts that are in either clause or sentence form: "We won the game; *however,* our star pitcher was injured"; "*However,* although we won the game, our star pitcher was injured."

Since these adverbs are relatively heavy, they are best suited for formal writing. When connecting two sentences, they are preceded by a semicolon and, except for the short adverbs (*also, hence, still, then*), are followed by a comma: "The meeting lasted for three hours; *finally,* it adjourned"; "It was raining; *hence* we decided to stay indoors"; "He took his seat; *then* he waited to be called." See SEMICOLON; THEN; TRANSITION.

Connotation/denotation are words that must be a part of every writer's vocabulary, especially *connotation,* for so often we use a word not for what it means, but for what it suggests. That which is *connoted,* then, is apart from its explicit, recognized meaning. Bear in mind that connotations may differ for everyone who reads or hears the word or phrase because what the word connotes—suggests, the picture that it raises in the mind—depends upon a person's education, experiences, and sense of value. No doubt the word *camp* has a different connotation for an American teenage boy from what it has for an adult German Jew who lived through World War II.

The connotations of *home* are *warmth, comfort, love,* and *security,* feelings associated with the word *home*. But the *denotation* of *home* is "a place where a person or family lives; a dwelling place," which is its exact, literal meaning, the meaning given in dictionaries.

Conscious refers to something perceived or felt *within* ourselves: a pain in the toe, a fear of the dark. We are **aware** of what is perceived *outside* of us: a waving red flag, a news broadcast. Thus, "I am *aware* of my neighbor's frustrations, but *conscious* of my own."

Consensus is spelled as given, not *concensus* (there's no "census" in *consensus*). Do not follow *consensus* with *of opinion,* since a consensus *is* a generally held opinion. Avoid the redundancy.

Consider, meaning *to regard as* or *to believe,* is not followed by *as*. We say, "We *consider* him the ideal student," not "*as* the ideal student"; "I *consider* her the epitome of grace," not "*as* the epitome of grace." This idiom also applies to *appoint, brand, elect,* and *name*. In "Stanton should have been appointed as district attorney," and in "Mickey was branded as a radical," *as* does not belong.

When, however, the meaning is *to give consideration to, to study, to examine, consider* is followed by *as*: "We will first *consider* him *as* a judge and then *as* a father"; "The novel *considers* him *as* an actor and *as* a politician." See REGARD.

Consist of/consist in are not interchangeable terms. *Consist of* means *to be made up of* and is followed by concrete nouns: "This alloy *consists of* bronze and nickel"; "My usual lunch *consists of* soup and a sandwich." *Consist in*, usually followed by an abstract noun, either points to a quality or ingredient possessed by something or introduces a definition. "The appeal of the play *consists in* its depiction of rural life"; "Truthfulness *consists in* being honest." See COMPRISE.

Contact (verb) meaning *to get in touch with, to communicate with*, is disliked by some authorities as being an informal term inappropriate to better speech and writing. But the word is catching on with many reputable writers, since to avoid it, with its all-embracing sense, one would have to say, "call, write, visit, or send your deputy," which means *get in touch*—and that too is what *contact* means. Fowler accepted it. He said, "Convenience has prevailed over prejudice." The probabilities are that most people will come to accept it.

Contemptible/contemptuous are not to be equated. A person who feels or shows contempt is *contemptuous*. Such a person is *disdainful*. He or she may show it by words or by a scornful look. A *contemptible* person or action is one deserving of contempt. Such a person may be a cheat or a liar.

Continual. See CONTINUOUS.

Continuous means *without interruption*, as in the way water flows from a faucet. **Continual** means *recurring periodically*, *repeated*, as in the way a telephone rings.

Convince means *to cause someone to believe*; **persuade**, *to cause someone to act*. A father may *convince* his son that his room needs straightening but be unable to *persuade* him to do anything about it. Idiomatically, a person can be convinced *that* something should be done or *of* the desirability of doing it. But strictly speaking a person may not be convinced *to do* something.

Idiom, and careful users of English, frown on an infinitive after *convince*, although using an infinitive is common in everyday usage. *Persuade* has no such problem. An infinitive may follow it on any level of English: "They *persuaded* him *to run* for office."

Copulative/linking verb—a verb that connects the subject with a predicate noun or pronoun or an adjective: "My uncle *was* a physician"; "We thought it *was* you"; "The waters *seem* clear."

What one should chiefly remember about copulative, or linking, verbs (the thing that causes the most common errors) is that they take adjectives, not adverbs: "I feel *bad*," not *badly*. See LINKING VERBS; PREDICATE NOMINATIVES.

Correlative conjunctions (those used in pairs)—*both . . . and, either . . . or, neither . . . nor, not only . . . but also, whether . . . or*—should be set out in parallel form. This means that if a noun or a verb or an adjectival phrase, or whatever, follows the first of the two conjunctions, the same form should follow the second. Rather than say, "I want *to visit* both Norway and *travel* in Sweden," make it "I want both *to visit* [infinitive] Norway and *to travel* [infinitive] in Sweden." In "No time has been set *either for* the meeting or the picnic," transpose *for* to precede *either* [*for either*]. "He *not only is* short but fat" should be rearranged: "He *is not only* short but fat." In many cases the simple repositioning of a preposition or a verb will make the sentence structurally balanced.

These conjunctions should not be used superfluously. For example, in "It is *both* rainy and [*and also*] windy" the sentence is just as clear and effective without *both*. And so *either* is unnecessary in "He may have *either* the red one or the blue one."

One thing more: A writer must decide whether the context requires *also* after *but* and *or not* after *whether*. Their use is not always mandatory. See EITHER/OR; NEITHER/NOR; WHETHER.

Couple, in precise English, is used to refer to *two persons or things joined or related in some way;* that is, *coupled,* as might be said of a married couple, two leashed golden retrievers, or a matched set of cuff links. In informal usage *couple* often replaces the numeral two. It is nevertheless better, since in such usage *couple* could also mean *few* or *several,* to say, "I bought *two* books today," rather than "*a couple of* books," especially if the books are on the English language. And do not omit *of* after *couple.* Not "We feel refreshed, since we slept a couple hours before dinner," but "slept a couple *of* hours before dinner."

If you start out by using *couple* as a singular, which you may ("The couple in the corner *is* the one we're looking for"), be consistent. Do not then say, "I think *they are* leaving now." You'll have to repeat *couple*: "I think the *couple is* leaving now." Writers who treat *couple* as a plural, and it is usually best to do so, avoid this kind of problem.

Credible means *worthy of belief* (*believable*). **Creditable** means *worthy of approval* (*praiseworthy*): "The jury found the testimony *credible* and the lawyer's summation *creditable*."

   Credulous is a distant cousin. It means *believing too easily, gullible*: "Where her brother is involved, Sophie is much too *credulous*. She believes everything he says."

Criteria, *standards of judgment,* is a plural word. Not "His *criteria* for the project *is* not based on sound advice," but "*are* not based on sound advice." Or recast: "His *criterion* for the project *is* . . ."

   Be not beguiled by the word *agenda*, a plural in Latin (meaning *things to be done*) that is treated as a singular in English. Its Latin singular form, *agendum*, has never been accepted into English. But the singular form *criterion* has been. It is the working singular of *criteria*. This means that *a criteria, one criteria,* and *the single criteria* are all wrong. Use *criterion* instead. See DATA.

Cupfuls. See -FUL.

D

Dangling participles (-*ing* words: *swimming, running*) do not relate logically to the sentence element they modify. To put it another way, these participles either have nothing to modify or have nothing that makes sense to modify. The reason, usually, is that the word that should be modified has been omitted.

Take as an example, "Coming around the bend, the courthouse was seen in all its glory." It was not the courthouse that was coming around the bend. We were. Make it "Coming around the bend, *we* saw the courthouse in all its glory." Or another: "Having missed my ride, it was too late for me to get to the meeting on time." To undangle, make it: "Having missed my ride, *I* was too late to get to the meeting on time." Still another: "Standing at the top of the stadium, the players below were clearly visible." The players obviously were not standing at the top of the stadium. They were below. Recast as: "Standing at the top of the stadium, *we* could clearly see the players below." In the rephrased sentences the modifiers have an appropriate word to modify, the first word in the main clause.

Consider another one, but with a different structure: "While on medical leave, my car was stolen." The car wasn't on medical leave. Correct by inserting a specific modifier into the *while* clause: "While *I* was on medical leave, my car was stolen." See PARTICIPLES.

Data, meaning *information,* especially to be used as a basis for analysis, is a plural noun. Therefore, "The data is incorrect" is incorrect. Make it "The *data are*" or, to avoid awkwardness, say, "The *items* in the data *are* incorrect."

Note, however, that some authorities treat *data* as a singular noun if only one item is involved and as a plural noun if more than one is involved. And note further that some usage critics regard *data* as a singular noun at all times and in all its uses. Considering the differences of opinion, it becomes the writer's decision which to follow. The plural sense of *data* is recommended here. See CRITERIA.

Dates from is used to indicate a span of time beginning with a particular date. Say, "His tenure *dates from* 1965," not "*dates back to* 1965."

Dates/times have no uniform styles. Tastes differ. Preferably capitalize *B.C.* and *A.D.,* but note *a.m.* and *p.m.* In "December 12, 1992, will be an unusual day," a comma follows *1992.* But in "*December 1992* is a good month to celebrate," no comma is used between the month and the year and certainly none after the year. In "*January 27* is my wife's natal day," note the cardinal number, not *January 27th.*

Deal is colloquial when used to mean *transaction,* as in "Armand completed a big *deal* in Baltimore." It is likewise colloquial when used to mean *under-*

handed arrangement ("The casino operators, you can be sure, made a *deal* with the commissioners") or *treatment* ("What an unfair *deal* that kid got").

In formal English *deal* is defined as *an act or round of apportioning or distributing*. It is often used in card games where it refers to the distribution of the playing cards.

Deeply. See PAST PARTICIPLE.

Deer. See SINGULAR AND PLURAL NOUNS.

Definitely. See ACTUALLY.

Delusion/illusion are similar in one sense in that each suggests *something that is not so*. The difference between them is that a *delusion* is a *false belief*, whereas an *illusion* is a *false impression*. A scarecrow gives the illusion of being a live person, but anyone who thinks it is alive is suffering from a delusion.

Denotation. See CONNOTATION.

Dependent clause. See SUBORDINATE CLAUSE.

Deprecate/depreciate are often mistaken for each other, even by educated persons. The thing to remember is that *depreciate* means *to belittle*. A person who depreciates his successes is a modest man. But more often the word is used to downgrade the successes of others, its sense being *to lessen in value*, which is what *belittle* or *disparage* means. To *deprecate* is *to express disapproval of, to protest or plead against*. Be aware that some dictionaries equate *deprecate* and *depreciate*, considering them synonyms simply because they look so much alike and are frequently interchanged, as in "Laura modestly *deprecated* [should be *depreciated*] her contribution." Which is no reason to adopt that viewpoint.

Depreciate. See DEPRECATE/DEPRECIATE.

Destroyed is a word often mistakenly modified. That which is destroyed is *demolished, ruined completely.* Therefore, avoid such phrases as *partially destroyed* or *completely destroyed.* Use *damaged* for the former and *destroyed* alone for the latter.

Diacritical markings. See ACCENT MARKS.

Diction is both the skillful use of words and the manner of pronouncing them. Those meanings are unrelated. If you're saying that a radio announcer's *diction* is in question, be sure, since the word has two senses, to see that the context clarifies the meaning.

Differ. See DIFFERENT.

Different idiomatically takes *from*, not *than*. One thing is different *from* another. Nevertheless, *different than* may be used when a clause follows—that is, when the words that follow have a subject and a verb: "The game was *different than* any of us could have imagined." This eliminates a wordy *from that which*: "The game was *different from that which* any of us could have imagined."

Guard against the unnecessary use of *different*. In "Two *different* musicians applied for the job," drop *different*, since naturally the two musicians were not the same person. And note the idiom *differ from* for a person or thing and *differ from* or *with* or *about* for an idea or opinion.

Dilemma is not a word meaning a problem or a distasteful situation. It means a *choice between two undesirable alternatives*, such as having to choose between communism and fascism.

Direct object. See TRANSITIVE VERBS.

Directions. See WEST.

Discover is said of something that has been found for the first time, something already in existence but previously unknown to man. For example, the Pacific Ocean was *discovered* by Balboa, but the ocean had been there before he arrived to see it. To **invent** is *to make up for the first time, to produce something new*. Medicines, by and large, are not discovered; they are invented. It might be said that *to invent* is *to come upon* and *to discover* is *to uncover*.

Disinterested means *impartial, unbiased*, as in the way a judge should be. **Uninterested** means *bored, not interested*. A person who knows no chemistry would most likely be uninterested in chemical formulas. These words, despite Webster, should not be interchanged. We should maintain the distinctive meaning of each one.

Dived, in formal language, is the acceptable form of the past tense of *dive*. **Dove** is informal and should be so confined. Which is not to say that "the quarterback *dove* for the ball" should be replaced by *dived*. By no means. In sports the form *dove* is solid, as it is common in everyday speech. Different words are appropriately used in different contexts.

Double negative. This expression refers to two negatives in a sentence that cancel each other: "He didn't do nothing"; "I don't know nothing about it." The objection to this construction is that the negatives reverse the meaning of the sentence by making an affirmative statement. The rule is that only one negative should be used to express a negative idea. But hold on. A sentence with two negatives that purposely cancel each other makes for acceptable English: "The plan is *not impossible*"; "The rookie is *not without* talent."

   Multiplication of negatives should be avoided, for they make a reader retrace steps to learn precisely what was meant. Consider "The project was thought to be *not only not impracticable* but *not* difficult to fund as well." Such sentences, when copy edited, should be revised. See BARELY/HARDLY/SCARCELY.

Double possessive, as in "Tom is a friend of my brother's," indicates that among my brother's friends, Tom is one. Or "I read a poem of Wordsworth's," meaning one of Wordsworth's poems. Using both the word with the apostrophe (the *inflected possessive*) and the *of* phrase (which then makes a double possessive) is idiomatically correct.

   The difference between a single and a double possessive is shown in the following examples: "This is a painting of Picasso" says that Picasso is the subject of the painting. "This is a painting of Picasso's" says that this is one of his paintings. "A story of Edward R. Murrow" is a story about Edward R. Murrow. "A story of Edward R. Murrow's" is a story by Edward R. Murrow.

Double prepositions, sometimes given other names by grammarians, may be correct ("John jumped *out of* the plane"; "The ball team came *over to* their opposition's dugout"), but often they are incorrect.

The word *of* after *off* is usually superfluous. Not "He leaped off of the pier," but "He leaped *off* the pier." Or substitute *from*: "He leaped *from* the pier." Not "I plan to meet him inside of an hour." Drop *of*. "He was *outside of* the building when the bell rang" also needs no *of*. And say, "The play is *over*," not *over with*. In "The batboy put the bats *up under* the canvas," *up* should be omitted. And AT ABOUT is an undesirable combination.

Caveat: Be sure to use *of* after *type* in such a sentence as, "He is the *type of* person I like," not "He is the *type* person I like."

Double titling should be avoided. Do not write, "We were addressed by *Dr.* Arthur Lamson, *M.D.*;" since the titles are repetitious. But "*Professor* Simon Tully, *D.D.S.*" is acceptable, since *D.D.S.* does not repeat the first title. See TITLES.

Doubt takes *that* in negative and interrogative sentences ("I do not *doubt that* you are right"; "Does anyone *doubt that* you are right?") and *whether* in positive statements: "I doubt *whether* he'll meet the deadline." Informally, *if* is used as often as *whether*, but most writers prefer *whether*: "I doubt *whether* [rather than *if*] he'll come." The same idiom governs *doubtful*.

Note: After an expression of doubting, *that* is required. Avoid *but that*: "We have no *doubt that* [not *but that*] everything will be as we predicted."

Doubtful. See DOUBT.

Dove. See DIVED.

Due to is best used only where it can replace *attributable to* or *caused by*, which usually is after a form of the verb *to be*: "His rapid advancement *was due to* [attributable to or caused by] concentrated effort and dedication." The phrase *due to* should not serve as an adverb, as in "*Due to* the rain, the game was postponed." Careful speakers and writers do not use *due to* to mean *because of*, as in the previous example. They would say, "*Because of* [owing to or on account of] the rain, the game was postponed."

Be aware that *due to* is so widely used as a preposition ("He went bankrupt *due to* carelessness") that such usage may come to be accepted for higher levels of English.

Due as an adjective (*due* process) and as a noun ("Give him his *due*") are not being considered here.

E

Each as the subject of a sentence is always followed by a singular verb and singular pronouns. Not "Each *have their* own briefcases" and "Each of the women *have their* own dryer," but "Each *has his* own briefcase" and "Each of the women *has her* own dryer." When *each* (as an adjective) modifies a compound subject—that is, two subjects joined by *and*—the dual subjects have no effect on the number of the verb, which remains singular: "Each senator and each legislator *has* endorsed the measure"; "Each book and each pamphlet *is* to be accounted for."

When *each* comes after a plural subject, the verb and pronoun should be plural: "Sally and Evelyn *each have their* personal vaults," not "Sally and Evelyn *each has her* ..."; "The men *each have their* own tool kits," not "The men *each has his*...." See BOTH; EVERY; EVERY ... EVERY; INDEFINITE PRONOUNS; PRONOUNS.

Each ... each. See EVERY ... EVERY.

Each other/one another, according to traditional rule, have distinctive uses. The first applies when two persons are involved; the second, when three or more: "Tom and Betty hugged *each other*"; "The senators from the New England states greeted *one*

55

another." Be aware, however, that in practice, especially in everyday speech, the rule is often ignored.

Effect. See AFFECT.

Either. See INDEFINITE PRONOUNS.

Either/or, neither/nor are followed by a verb form whose number must agree with the nearer noun: "Either the students or the *teacher is* to control the Student Council"; "Either the teacher or the *students are* to control the Student Council." "The faculty or *I am* to escort the Dean"; "The faculty or *we are* to escort the Dean." Note that plain *or* follows the same convention: "Grapes or an orange *is* what we want"; "An apple or grapes *are* what we want."

The alternatives suggested by these conjunctions should be in structural balance, a convention called *parallelism.* Not "The soldiers wanted *either to have better food* or more leave time," but "The soldiers wanted to have *either better food* or more leave time." See CORRELATIVE CONJUNCTIONS.

Elect. See CONSIDER.

Ellipsis is *an omission of a word or words.* When confronted with a comparison in which there are omitted words, spell out the sentence, mentally, to arrive at the correct form of the pronoun. For example, in "Sammy likes Betty more than I," *do* is implied ("more than I *do*"). But *me* would be as correct as *I,* depending on the meaning intended. Consider: "Sammy likes Betty more than me." There, *he likes* is implied ("more than *he likes* me"). The case of the pronoun is the key to the correct meaning.

Words that are essential should of course not be omitted. For example, "This dessert is as good if not better than that one" requires *as* after *good*. "This boat is speedier than any in Cape Cod" requires *other* after *any*. In "They either have or will decide when to move," *decided* is needed after *have*. See AS; COMPARATIVE FORMS OF ADJECTIVES; OMISSION OF WORDS.

Else should be followed by *than*, not by *but*: "It is nothing else *than* [not *but*] fear." In "No one else but her," *else* is redundant and should be omitted: "No one *but* her." See COMPARATIVE FORMS OF ADJECTIVES.

Elude. See ALLUDE/REFER.

Emerge/immerge are as confusing in practice as two words can be, even though their meanings are distinctive. *Emerge* means *to rise out of*, as in "The submarine *emerged* right before our eyes." *Immerge* has an opposite meaning, *to disappear, to plunge into*: "The dog *immerged* into the darkness of the night." Figuratively, a person can immerge himself in his studies, but *immerse* is the more common word: "She *immersed* herself in academic studies."

Note that *emerge* has one *m*, whereas *immerge* has two.

English is generally divided into three categories, although all authorities do not agree with that number. *Standard English*, which is of the highest level, is often called *formal English*. It is the English used in documents, theses, and so forth. The level below it is called *informal English*, which incorporates *colloquial English*, that which is used every day in conversation and in writing. Below that is slang or *vulgar English*.

Enormity *means excessive wickedness, heinousness*, something monstrously evil: "The *enormity* of this mass murder shocked the entire community." **Enormousness** is used of size. It means huge: "The *enormousness* of our new college stadium made us gasp in delight."
  Be careful with this one. Some writers and many politicians unconcernedly use *enormity* where *enormousness* belongs. Do not follow suit. If the amphitheater is *enormous*, do not speak of its *enormity*. That would make no sense.

Enthuse is a back-formation from *enthusiasm* and means *to show enthusiasm*. Its use should be confined to informal contexts. In formal discourse say, "He is *enthusiastic* [or spoke *enthusiastically*] about his prospects," not "He is *enthused* about his prospects."

Entomology/etymology are two easily confused terms. The first is *the study of insects;* the second embraces *the derivation of words, their origin and history.*

Equally needs no accompanying *as*. In "This material is equally as good," omit either *as* or *equally*, preferably *as* because *equally* is more emphatic. When these words are used together, the phrase is redundant.

Note that when two persons or things are being compared, *as* is the word to use: "Carlotta dances *as* well as Melissa." Not *equally*.

Equivocal. See AMBIGUOUS/EQUIVOCAL.

Erotic. See EXOTIC/EROTIC/ERRATIC.

Erratic. See EXOTIC/EROTIC/ERRATIC.

Estimated should not be used with *about* in the same sentence (*"estimated* to be worth *about* four thousand dollars"). *About* is redundant; drop it, since both *about* and *estimated* carry the idea of *approximation*.

Etc. is an abbreviation of the Latin *et cetera* ("and other things"). It indicates that a list is only partly complete.

Always follow *etc.* with a period, and also a comma if the sentence continues ("I read mysteries, romances, *etc.*, but not biographies"). Do not precede *etc.* with *and* (*et* in Latin means *and*) and do not use *etc.* if the list begins with *such as* or *for example*.

Informal writing accepts *etc.*, but formal style prefers *and so forth* or *and so on*.

Etymology. See ENTOMOLOGY/ETYMOLOGY.

Even. See ADVERBS.

Ever. See ADVERBS.

Every follows the same conventions as those that govern EACH; that is, when *every* introduces a sentence, it is a singular adjective, modifying a singular noun, and is followed by a singular verb. Therefore, not "Every one of them suit me fine," but "Every *one* of them *suits* me fine." Related pronouns are also singular: "Every *teacher has* been requested to prepare *his* or *her* analysis."

Beware of those constructions that make for awkwardness when the subject indicates a plural sense but nevertheless requires a singular verb. The sentence "Every person seemed happy with the choice, but was he being honest?" is not only cumbersome but misleading. The sense of that sentence is that a number of persons were involved. Using *they* for *he* (and converting *was* to *were*) would be logical but grammatically incorrect. The easy solution is to replace *every* with a plural word: "*All those* present seemed happy with the choice, but were *they* being honest?" See EACH; EVERY . . . EVERY; INDEFINITE PRONOUNS; SEXISM.

Every . . . and every, as in "*Every* boy and *every* girl has to report for art class," ignores *and* and takes a singular verb. This principle applies even when the second *every* is omitted: "*Every* question and [every] answer *was* clearly heard." Using the redundant *each and every* does not change the number of the verb. A singular is still required.

Using *each . . . and each* instead of *every . . . and every* makes no change in the rules governing the number of the verb and referents. They are required to be singular. See EACH; INDEFINITE PRONOUNS.

Everyone is not. See EVERYTHING IS NOT.

Everyplace. See ANYPLACE.

Everything is not is a common misusage, as in "Everything is not the way it should be." The sentence must be reworded—"*Not everything is* the way it should be"—unless the thought is that *nothing* is the way it should be.

Everyone is not also is not acceptably worded. Rather than "Everyone is not in agreement with the plan," say, "*Not everyone* is in agreement with the plan."

Everywhere. See ANYPLACE.

Evidently. See APPARENTLY.

Exactly. See ADVERBS.

Except. See ACCEPT.

Exotic/erotic/erratic sound so much alike that it is no wonder they are sometimes confused. *Exotic* means *strange;* that is, something from another part of the world. But it has also come to mean *strikingly and charmingly different. Erotic* refers to *sexual love and desire.* Its synonym is *amatory. Erratic* means *having no regular or prescribed course.* It is generally used to mean *unpredictable.*

Expect. See ANTICIPATE.

Expletives. See IT.

F

The fact that is a wordy substitute for *that*: *"The fact that* I enjoy Switzerland is bound to make me want to return" could read: *"That* I enjoy Switzerland is bound to make me want to return." Or, rephrased even without *that*: "An enjoyable visit to Switzerland is bound to make me want to return."

The fact should not be used superfluously, as in "The analysis pointed out [*the fact*] that several units should be closed."

Before using *in spite of the fact that*, consider *although*; and before using *due to the fact that*, consider *because*.

Famous should not be used when **notorious** is meant. Although both words refer to someone who has received widespread notice, their applications are different. In fact, their meanings are quite opposite. *Famous* refers to someone in good repute; *notorious* refers to someone who is well known in an unfavorable sense. Be careful of this latter word. *Notorious* is sometimes mistakenly used for *famous*; seldom is the reverse true.

Fantastic. See ADVERBS.

Farther is used of physical distance: "We traveled *farther* than we had expected." It is the comparative of *far*. The sense of **further** is *to a greater degree*, and it is used in all other cases: "We shall study this matter *further*."

Feel bad/badly. See COPULATIVE VERBS.

Feet/foot. See SINGULAR AND PLURAL NOUNS.

Few. See INDEFINITE PRONOUNS.

Fewer is used of *countable* things or persons (*fewer* houses, *fewer* books, *fewer* people). **Less** is used when one is speaking of *inseparable quantity*, usually something in bulk or mass, things that are measured (*less* gravel, *less* time, *less* money). *Fewer* is used as a modifier of plural nouns ("We have *fewer friends* since we *were* graduated"); *less*, of singular nouns ("*Less sugar is* better for you"). *Less* is used when the reference is to periods of time, sums of money, and measures of distance and weight. "It took *less* than five minutes to find the answer"; "He had *less* than ten dollars"; "The box weighed *less* than four pounds." See WEIGHTS, MONEY, AND MEASUREMENTS.

Finalize is a controversial word. Although it has been used by some prominent persons, it has been rejected by many others. Prefer *make final, complete, conclude,* or some other suitable expression and avoid criticism from any source, including all the Maury Maverick followers. Maverick was a congressman from Texas during World War II. His listing of pretentious words, called *Gobbledygook Memorandum,* words that must be avoided, included *finalize.*

The advice here is never to add *-ize* to a noun to produce a verb. Such coinages sound offensive to many sensitive ears. This means that, although some useful words ending in *-ize* have been fully welcomed into the good graces of English (*fertilize, fraternize, harmonize, summarize*), new creations (*optimize, prioritize, radicalize*—and *finalize*) are resented and deplored by careful users of English.

Finished, in formal usage, is preferred to *through* in such a sentence as "The lecturer *has finished* [rather than *is through with*] his introductory remarks."

First/second/third are preferable to *firstly, secondly,* and *thirdly*. Some writers, however, prefer *first, secondly,* and *thirdly,* but almost no one uses *firstly*.

Cardinal numbers (those that indicate quantity: 1, 2, 3, etc.), and ordinal numbers (those that indicate order: first, second, etc.), when in sequence, should follow this example: "The *first three* chapters will be reviewed tomorrow," not *the three first.* There cannot logically be three first chapters.

Fish. See SINGULAR AND PLURAL NOUNS.

Flammable/inflammable are exact synonyms. Both mean *burnable*. Something that will not burn is *nonburnable* or *noncombustible*. But note that when the sense is *easily angered or excited,* only *inflammable* is correct: "There was an *inflammable* confrontation between two Arab states." And note further that a speech that tends to inflame is said to be *inflammatory*.

Flaunt means *to boast, to show off, to display ostentatiously*, as in the way some dowagers drape themselves in jewelry. **Flout** means *to mock*, or *to defy, to treat with disdain or contempt*, the way some corrupt politicians treat the law. Be particularly careful of *flaunt*. It is often misused for *flout*. A person who shows contemptuous disregard for the law doesn't *flaunt* it; he *flouts* it.

For is preferable to *in the amount of* in "He drew a check *for* four hundred dollars." Economy in words is a virtue. See BECAUSE.

Forbear is a verb meaning *to desist* or *to refrain from*. It is also a noun meaning *ancestor*. Unlike the word *forbear*, **forebear** is not a verb; it is only a noun, and its meaning is *ancestor*. Confused? Resolve the problem by using *forebear* (with its two *e*'s) when an ancestor is meant. Use *forbear* as a verb only.

Forbid to. See IDIOM.

Forebear. See FORBEAR.

Foreseeable future. See NEAR FUTURE/THE NOT TOO DISTANT FUTURE.

For example. See THAT IS.

For instance. See THAT IS.

Former/latter are direct opposites. They should be used only of two units—the *former*, the first of two; the *latter*, the second of two: "I prefer the *former* to the *latter*"; "The *latter* of these choices is inferior to the *former*." If more than two persons or things are involved, use *first* or *first-named* and *last* and *last-named*: "Vincent, Charles, and Fred attended the meeting. The *first-named* gave an interesting talk"; "I want the *last-named* person in the roll call to step up front."

Be sure that these designations clearly indicate the items to which each refers. Since these terms can confuse, be wary.

Fortuitous means *accidental, happening by chance.*
Fortunate means *lucky, having good fortune.* Fortuitously meeting your New York college roommate in Chicago is fortunate. Fortuitously meeting your New York parole officer in Chicago, when you're in violation of parole, is not fortunate. It most likely will turn out to be unfortunate.

For you to ordinarily should not follow a verb. In "We want *for you to* leave early," *for* does not belong. But the phrase is correctly used immediately after a noun ("Salvatore set up a *meeting for you to* be interviewed") or an adjective ("Angie would be *delighted for you to* visit her").

Founder. See SINK.

Fraction is a mathematical term meaning *a part of the whole.* In general discourse a fraction is assumed to be a *small* part. But this assumption might not be justified; a fraction could be a large part. Therefore, to be precise, *fraction* should not be equated with *small* or *little*, although only a purist would consider the world *fraction* to mean anything other than *a small part.* To avoid any misunderstanding, unlikely though it be, modify *fraction* with *small, tiny,* or *little,* unless, of course, a large part is being considered. The expression *only a fraction* is always taken to represent a small part.

Fragments (words lacking an independent subject and predicate), although seldom appropriate in formal writing, may be used in informal writing, but even there only sparingly and where suitable. Try one. Like this one.

Some fragments, although technically unfinished, can stand by themselves. "Well, I never," is a clear sign of astonishment, and "On the contrary" indicates disagreement. It is unlikely that anyone would misunderstand them.

-ful is a singular ending (*basketful*); **-fuls,** a plural (*handfuls, cupfuls, bucketfuls*). There is no such word as *handsful. Three spoons full* refers to different spoons that have been filled. *Three spoonfuls* means one spoon filled three times. We say, "Take two *spoonfuls* of medicine daily," but "On the table are six *cups full* of sugar." The first implies a measure; the second, separate cups.

Fulsome has become standard political jargon through its use in the phrase *fulsome praise.* Politicians who use it think they are being complimentary. They're not. *Fulsome* does not mean *generous, hearty,* or *abundant.* It means *excessive* or *insincere.* The politicians' *fulsome praise* is so lavish as to have a false ring. The best thing to say about this word is to forget it.

Further. See FARTHER.

Future perfect tense is used to indicate that an action or event will be completed at some definite time in the future. It is formed by adding *have* to *shall* or *will* to the future tense: "By next week I *shall have saved* enough money before the bill comes due"; "Stuart *will have finished* his studies by nine o'clock."

Although this tense is seldom used (and some grammars pay scant attention to it), it is useful, even necessary, in some sentences. It should not be forgotten.

G

Gender, as applied to English grammar, indicates the sex of a noun or pronoun. There are four genders: *masculine, feminine, common,* and *neuter. Masculine* denotes the male sex and *feminine* the female. The *common* sex may denote either sex (*child, baby, adolescent, adult*). *Neuter* denotes the absence of sex (*chair, table, tree*).

General/permanent truths (facts generally acknowledged as unchangeable) are expressed in the present tense, even if a verb in the past tense preceded: "He *said* [past tense] that honesty *is* [present tense] the best policy"; "We all *learned* [past tense] that water *freezes* [present tense] at thirty-two degrees Fahrenheit." This use of a past and a present tense in the same sentence runs counter to the rule that the tense of verbs should not conflict; for example, "Walt *testified* that he *lived* in Havertown," even though he still lives there.

Genitive is the possessive case of a noun modifier: the *boy's* gloves, the *woman's* pocketbook. It is not necessary to know this grammatical term to write or speak well. But some books may use it instead of the word *possessive,* so it's good to know.

Gerunds are verbal nouns that end in -*ing.* Said in another way, they are verb forms that function as nouns. The noun or pronoun that modifies a gerund must be in the possessive case. Therefore, not "The boss did not like the boy dancing in the office," but *the boy's dancing*. The boss did not dislike the boy. He disliked his dancing in the office. Not "My mother objected to Mary bringing her dog into the living room," but to *Mary's bringing* her dog into the living room. Here again, the objection was not to Mary, but to her bringing her dog into the living room.

The possessive case, as in the examples cited above, immediately precedes the gerund. If the noun or pronoun that would be made possessive does not immediately precede the gerund—that is, if words intervene—the possessive is not used. Although we say, "The pianist missed several notes without the *conductor's noticing* it," we say, "The pianist, without the *conductor* or anyone else *noticing* it, missed several notes."

An afterthought: A gerund may serve as a subject of a sentence ("*Swimming* is my favorite sport") or as an object ("He loves *swimming*").

Good (adjective) should not replace *well* (adjective and adverb) after the LINKING VERBS *feel, look,* or *seem.* As used here, *well* is what is called a *predicate adjective* (an adjective that follows a linking verb). A person who feels, looks, or seems well is apparently in good health: "I'm happy to say I feel *well.*" Since *feel* also serves as an active verb, it may be modified by *well,* but there it functions as an adverb: "The blind man *feels* his way cautiously and *well.*"

When the adjective *good* is linked to the subject by *feel,* the reference is to bodily sensations. And when linked by *look,* it does not refer to health; it refers to appearance: "It *looks good* enough to eat"; "She *looks good* in sport clothes." See WELL.

Goodwill/good will/good-will are synonymous terms, yet they are often used differently. Hyphenated *good-will* serves only as an adjective: "It was a *good-will* gesture." The phrase *good will* usually appears in an agreement of sale of a business: "The seller believes the *good will* of his business is being understated." The one-word *goodwill* may be used in either case, as an adjective or as a noun.

Got is such an abused verb that it would take pages to list its common misusages. The Pennsylvania license plate in the 1980's sported the motto: "You've got a friend in Pennsylvania," which raised a grammatical furor among the local gentry. Interestingly, some usage critics condone that phraseology, saying that *have got* is an emphatic form of *have.* But many critics do not go along with that thinking. They say that *have* is all that is necessary. Certainly, "*Have* you a dictionary?" sounds better than "Have you *got* a dictionary?"

Graduate (verb) is best used in the active form. "He *graduated from* college yesterday," rather than "He *was graduated from* college yesterday." But this is not to say that the passive form is objectionable, just that the active form is preferred. Note that the key word in either phrasing is *from.* Which means that a sentence such as "He graduated college yesterday" should be recast *graduated from* or *was graduated from.*

Greatly. See PAST PARTICIPLES.

H

Had better is idiomatic. *Better had* is an improper, reversed twosome. We say, "I *had better* get to school on time." Those who say, "I *better had* get to school on time" had better get there to learn the correct idiom.

Had of. See OF.

Had ought is an unacceptable combination. Not "The dean had ought to think more about us." Omit *had*. Equally bad is the contracted form *we'd* with *ought*, as in "*We'd ought* to go."

The similar combinations—*had have* and *had of*—also do not properly go together. Not "I wish I *had have* [or *had of*] gone." Those pairs contain unnecessary baggage. Unload. Use *had* alone: "I wish I *had* gone."

Half is singular or plural, depending on the sense of the following *of* phrase: "Half of the money *has* been spent"; "At least half of her remarks *were* uncalled for." Stay clear of *a half of a* or *a half of an*. You may properly ask for either *a half loaf* or *half a loaf* (the former is preferable), but not *a half of a loaf*. And note that, although *cut in halves* is technically correct, the general preference is for *cut in half*.

Handfuls. See -FUL.

Hanged is the preferred word to mean *death by hanging.* In other senses, use **hung.** A person is *hanged;* a picture is *hung.*

Hardly. See BARELY/HARDLY/SCARCELY.

Have got. See GOT.

Have got to is a colloquial expression for *must, should,* or *ought to.* "*I have got to* have my car repaired" in serious writing should be rephrased "I *must* [or *should*] have my car repaired." And "*I have got to* prepare this report" needs amending: "I *ought to. . . .*"

But note that *have got* is acceptable phrasing when it means *obtained:* "I *have* already *got* a partner." See GOT.

Headquarters is a plural noun when it refers to place—"The headquarters *are* in Nashville"—but a singular when it refers to authority: "Headquarters *has* issued new orders." *Headquarter* as a verb, although listed in some dictionaries, is frowned upon by many writers and usage critics. Avoid "The company is *headquartered* in Knoxville." Say, instead, "The company's *headquarters* are in Knoxville."

Healthy means *possessing good health* (*healthy* people). **Healthful** means *giving* or *producing health* (*healthful* foods). More and more *healthy* is being used in the sense of *healthful,* especially where climate is concerned. In fact *healthy climate* (often seen in travel brochures) is a phrase approaching idiomatic acceptance. Nevertheless, despite the frequency of this loose usage, precision and clarity call for *healthful* where *conducive to good health* is meant. No one can fault you for using words correctly.

Help. See BUT WHAT.

Her. See POSSESSIVE NOUNS.

Here. See THERE.

Historic/historical. See A/AN.

Home is a peculiar word in that sometimes it needs an accompanying *at* and sometimes not. The rule is that *at* should precede *home* whenever the verb in the sentence is static. We should therefore say, "Al *stayed at home* last night," not "Al *stayed home* last night." Rather than "Agnes *was home* when you called," make it, "Agnes *was at home.* . . ." But note that when you say, "Tom walked home after school," no *at* is required because there *home* is an adverb.

Hopefully, an adverb, means *in a hopeful manner.* A person may say, "Hopefully, the defendant awaited the jury's verdict" because the defendant was full of hope. But it is incorrect to say, "Hopefully, the train will arrive on time." A train cannot arrive full of hope. It is just as easy, and correct at the same time, to say, "I hope that" or "It is hoped that." Unlike *regrettably* and other such adverbs, *hopefully,* as a sentence adverb, has not been admitted into standard English.

Make note that the frequent use of *hopefully* (a less cumbersome alternative to "it is to be hoped that" and a less personal alternative to "*I* [or *we*] hope that") is weakening the strong stand against it by some word usage authorities.

Hours. See A.M./P.M.

However. See CONJUNCTIVE ADVERBS.

Human, a word that was once used as an adjective only, is increasingly being used as a noun—to the point that many dictionaries now recognize it as a variant of *human being.* Traditionally, a person was known as a *human being.* But many reputable writers have now come to refer to a person simply as a *human.* Which is not to say that the full designation—*human being*—is not to be preferred. Certainly it sounds more dignified.

Hung. See HANGED.

Hyphens are important punctuation devices, but since punctuation is not an integral part of this book, one must look elsewhere for guidelines and governing rules. But two special situations deserve attention here.

The adjective *so-called,* which implies doubt or sarcasm, is hyphenated when it precedes a noun—"The *so-called financier* had no money for bus fare"—but not when it follows a noun: "He is our *angel, so called.*" Note that the nouns were not enclosed in quotation marks.

Up to date, meaning *abreast of the times,* follows the same convention. It is hyphenated when it precedes a noun—"It is an *up-to-date system*"—but not when it follows a noun: "This brings your *payment up to date.*"

To come back to *so-called*: Just as neither quotation marks nor italics were used with *so called* (see the example), so expressions introduced by *called*, *known as*, *named*, and *referred to* are treated in the same way.

I

-ics is an ending of a word that may be either singular or plural, depending on its use. For example, "Ethics *is* a governing standard among decent people"; "Their ethics *are* questionable"; "The acoustics here *are* overrated"; "Acoustics *is* the science of sound." The rule here is that the *-ics* words referring to a *science* or *a branch of study* are regularly singular: "Although civics *is* an important course, physics *is* more interesting"; "Gymnastics *is* a field we should embrace." Those same *-ics* words referring to a *set of principles* or to *concrete activities or practices,* and so forth, are treated as plurals: "The athletics here *are* for everyone"; "The mechanics of linguistics *are* difficult to master."

Idiom is an established form of expression that is not necessarily in accord with the senses of the words it contains. For example, "Many a man has tried and lost" isn't grammatically feasible, since *many* refers to more than one and *a* refers to one only. Or consider "She *makes* friends easily." Some idioms are informal, such as "He was left with *egg on his face.*" Some are accepted on any level of English: "My uncle is *the salt of the earth.*" Much idiom consists of the way words are put together to convey properly ideas or information. For example, *hardly . . . when* is proper and not *hardly . . . than*, as is *forbid to* and not *forbid from*.

For those who may be seeking a more precise definition, the following is the one set out by *Webster*: "an expression established in the usage of language that is peculiar to itself either in grammatical construction (as *no, it wasn't me*) or in having a meaning that cannot be derived as a whole from the conjoined meanings of its elements (as *Monday week* for 'the Monday a week after next Monday'; *how are you* for 'what is the state of your health or feelings?')."

If, when followed by *might* or *could* to indicate conditional ability, needs a following *should* or *would*, not *shall* or *will*: "If the news *might* disturb him, I *would* not [not *will not*] tell him."

If is preferable to *in the event* (of). "*If* it doesn't shower, we'll go" rather than "*In the event* it doesn't shower, we'll go."

If and when. See CANNOT AND WILL NOT.

If/whether are not to be interchanged in better speech or writing. Using *if* in certain contexts may be confusing. "Let Horace know *if* the book is satisfactory" says that Horace is to be informed *if* (but *only* if) the book is satisfactory. Otherwise, not. When *whether* replaces *if*, the meaning becomes that Horace is to be informed one way or the other; that is, to be told that the book is suitable or to be told that it is unsuitable.

A good guideline is to use *whether* (instead of *if*) if the words *or not* can be inserted: "Jack wondered *whether* [*or not*] the movers would arrive as promised." But in "I wonder what would happen *if* it rained during the picnic," no alternatives are involved; hence *if*.

Note the following: *whether* is required when it begins a sentence ("*Whether* it is Monday or Tuesday . . ."), follows a preposition ("The problem *of whether* . . . ," or, without *of*: "The problem *whether* . . ."), or follows the verb *to be* ("The problem *is whether* . . ."). See DOUBT; WHETHER.

If they had/if they would have are constructions so frequently misused that they require special attention. Do not say, "If they lived ten years longer, everything might be changed today." Make it "If they *had* lived ten years longer. . . ." And not "If she would have written me, I should have replied immediately," but "If she *had* written me. . . ." It is correct to say, "If they *had been* more thoughtful (but they weren't), they might have helped us in our time of need." And "If Tom *had asked* his boss (but he didn't), he would have been given leave time." Notice that *had*, not *would have* (a future form), is used in the *if* clause.

Illusion. See DELUSION/ILLUSION.

Immerge. See EMERGE/IMMERGE.

Immerse. See EMERGE/IMMERGE.

Impeach is not synonymous with *convict*. If Nixon had been impeached, he could not on that basis alone have been removed from office, fined, or jailed. *To impeach* is to bring charges against a person so as to have him removed from office. The word's sense is *to accuse*, not *to remove*.

Imperative mood. See MOOD.

Imply/infer are frequently misused words, one for the other. The culprit in this twosome usually is *infer*. Seldom is *imply* misused.

To *imply* is *to hint at, to suggest*—that is, to make no explicit statement. To *infer* is to surmise or deduce, to derive by reasoning. A speaker implies; his audience infers. To put it another way, the implier is the pitcher and the inferrer is the catcher. This means that it is a mistake to say, "Do you mean to *infer* I'm all wrong?"

Importantly, in such a sentence as "Thomas immediately turned the business around; more *importantly*, he saved its life," is preferably replaced by *important*. The omitted construction is *what is more important*, the sense being that the life of the business was more important than its immediate turnaround. However, the use of *importantly* by some writers is far from uncommon. But do not prefer it.

Inaugurate. See BEGIN.

In behalf of. See BEHALF.

Include/including do not mean that what follows is a complete list of all items or members. *Include* is wrongly used of, say, a plan of four items if the plan consists of only four items. A proper word would be *comprise*. Of course, if the plan consists of more than four items, *include*, which indicates that at least one member is unnamed, would be correct.

A series that begins with *includes* should not end with *and others*. Not "The guest list includes the Golds, the McClatchys, the Brownsteins, and others." Omit *and others* and insert *and* after *McClatchys*.

Incredible/incredulous have a similar basic sense of *unbelief*. That which is *incredible* is *unbelievable*. It may be a story, a book, or an account of a happening. A person who is *unbelieving* is *incredulous*. You might say, "The tale David told of his escape was *incredible*, and, I must say, it left us all *incredulous*."

In general conversation *incredible* is frequently used to mean *almost* unbelievable; not that it can't be believed, but that it is hard to believe. See ADJECTIVES.

Indefinite pronouns—*anyone, each, either, everyone, neither, someone*, but not NONE—always take a singular verb and singular pronouns: "*Each appears* to be what *his* promoter had hoped for"; "*Neither* of the schedules *is* appealing."

Compound pronouns with *any, every, some*, and *no* also are always singular: "*Everyone knows he* should be polite at all times"; "*Anybody is* welcome."

Both, few, many, others, and *several* are always plural: "*Few are* here, but *others are* coming."

The pronouns *all, most*, and *some* take a singular or a plural verb depending on whether a singular or plural sense is understood: "*All* the money *is* lost, but *all* the books *have been* saved"; "*Some* of his energy *has* waned"; "*Some* of the tires *are* worn." See ANYONE/ANY ONE; EACH; EVERY ... EVERY; NONE; POSSESSIVE PRONOUNS; PRONOUNS.

Independent clause. See SUBORDINATE CLAUSE.

Indicative mood. See MOOD.

Indirect object names *the person or thing to which something is given, said, shown, or done.* Although the term may be unimportant, the construction and functioning of an indirect object are not. An indirect object usually precedes the direct object: "Read *him* [indirect object] the *letter* [direct object]. No preposition (*to* or *for*) is used, but one is implied: "Read [*to*] him the letter." If the indirect object follows the direct object, it is introduced by *to* or *for*, whichever is appropriate: "I bought a present *for* her."

The indirect object follows such verbs as *buy, get, give, lend, make, offer, pay, read, send, show,* and *write*: "Send *him* the plans"; "Show *me* your new shirt"; "Make *us* an offer."

Indirect quotations (quotations that paraphrase or summarize) usually follow *said* or, less often, *said that.* They call for *should* or *would*, not *shall* or *will*: "It was reported that Roberts *said* he *would* not go."

Note that the quotation is capitalized in "The newscaster said, '*The* worst is over,' " but not in "The newscaster said *that the* worst is over." And no special punctuation is needed.

Individual person is a foolish combination of words. Avoid it. Each person is an individual. Therefore, do not say, "Each *individual person* is to be examined," although you may say, "Each person is to be examined individually"; that is, not in a group. If a contrast is being made between a person and a group, it is proper to say, "The only individual who objected was Thomas Wright," but even there *person* would be a better choice.

Infer. See IMPLY.

Infinitives are verb forms that are preceded by *to*—either expressed, "We were happy *to* learn that you passed your test," or implied, "My neighbor helped [*to*] move the sofa."

The pronoun following an infinitive is almost always in the objective case to agree with its subject, which is also in the objective case (this sounds contradictory because subjects are usually in the nominative case). This point may be illustrated in the sentence "The delegates thought *us* to be *them* (*them* is an objective-case form agreeing with the subject *us*). And not, "The best way for you and *I* to go is according to the rules," but "for you and *me* to go." See SPLIT INFINITIVES.

Inflammable. See FLAMMABLE.

Initiate. See BEGIN.

Innovation refers to something new. Therefore, *new innovation* is redundant, as redundant as *advance planning*. No one plans backwards.

In order to consists, in almost all cases, of two unnecessary words—the first two. Rather than "He planned the itinerary in order to get all the benefits possible," drop *in order*, leaving the less cluttered "He planned the itinerary carefully *to* get all the benefits possible."

Inside of. See DOUBLE PREPOSITIONS.

Intensive pronouns. See REFLEXIVE PRONOUNS.

Interesting. See ADJECTIVES.

Interjections, in grammar, are *emotional expressions that have no grammatical relationships*. Their only purpose is to express a strong feeling such as disgust, happiness, or enthusiasm. Common interjections are *Oh!*; *Baa!*; *Heavens!*; *Alas!*; *Hey!*; *Ho!*; *Horrors!*

Intervening words or phrases between subject and verb have no effect on the number of the verb: "The reason for his writings *was* [not *were*] to raise funds for his favorite charity." And not "The primary goals of the Aberdeen High School was to raise reading levels," but "*were* to raise reading levels." See AS WELL AS; PARENTHETICAL ELEMENTS; VERBS.

Into/in to are not interchangeable terms. *Into* is a preposition with a variety of meanings, of which the most common is *to go inside*: "We all went *into* the courtroom." *In to* (two words) is an adverb and preposition combination, the adverb coalescing with some specific verbs: "Essie *went in* to get a drink of water"; "José *went in* to eat dinner."

Be careful of *into*. It has become a vogue word, as in "My son is *into* computers." Prefer *interested in*, *devoted to*, or *busy with*.

Intransitive verbs take no object: "Please *stand* quietly"; "I will be *sitting* all afternoon." Some verbs can function as either a transitive verb—"I escaped the terrorists"—or an intransitive verb—"I escaped from the terrorists." The point is that it depends on how the verb is used. To restate the principle: If an object follows the verb, the verb is transitive ("He bats the *ball*"); if no object follows, the verb is intransitive ("He bats poorly"). See TRANSITIVE VERBS.

Invent. See DISCOVER.

Invite should be used only as a verb, never as a noun. Do not say, "We sent them an *invite*." Use *invitation*.

Irregardless is not a word in the English language, regardless of how many people use it. Or, as was said, regardless of the school of a-word-is-a-word-if-the-people-use-it. Avoid. Use *regardless*.

Is when/is where. See WHERE.

It is a filler word when it begins a sentence that has a delayed subject. For example, in "*It* is painful for him to learn these things," the real subject is not *it* but the infinitive phrase, as becomes clear when the sentence is transposed and the *it* removed: "*To learn these things* is painful for him." Take another: "*It* is important that you help her now." Transposed, and without the *it*, the sentence reads: *"That you help her now* is important." The italicized words are the true subject.

Notice that the pattern of *it*, called an *expletive* or an *anticipatory subject*, is always the same: *it is*. But although the phrase is singular, it may be followed by either a singular or a plural noun: "It is my *friend* I'm concerned about"; "It is my *friends* I'm concerned about."

Avoid using the expletive *it* and the pronoun *it* in the same sentence, as in "*It* is cold when *it* snows, but when *it* melts, *it* becomes warm." See THERE.

It goes without saying. See NEEDLESS TO SAY.

Its is the possessive form of *it*: "The French poodle is feeding *its* puppies." Like other possessive personal pronouns—*his, hers, yours, theirs*—*its* has no apostrophe. *It's* with an apostrophe is a contraction of *it is*—"*It's* time for lunch"—or *it has*: "*It's* been a long time since I've seen you." Therefore, not "The car got *it's* hood painted today." Be not deceived into thinking that *it's*, because it has an apostrophe, is a possessive form. It's not.

It's me. See ME; TO BE.

"-ize" words. See FINALIZE.

J

Jargon, as the word is mostly used today, refers to *the technical language of a science, trade, or profession.* Jargon should be avoided in ordinary speech and writing in favor of plain English, English that can be read and understood by laypeople and the general public.

Jibe/gibe means *jeer* or *mock, taunt,* or *deride.* The spellings are variants and the meanings are interchangeable. But when used informally to mean *to agree* or *to be in harmony with,* only *jibe* is correct. *Jibe* is also a nautical term, but it is not being considered here.

Jury. See COLLECTIVE NOUNS.

Just is redundant in *just exactly*: "It is *just exactly* three o'clock." Choose either *just* or *exactly.* Equally to be avoided is the expression *just about,* since *just* indicates precision and *about* approximation.

When *just* refers to the recent past, it is used with a perfect tense (one with *have* or *had*), not with the past tense. Say, "They *have just* landed at the airport," not "They *just landed* at the airport." See ADVERBS.

Just as. See EQUALLY.

K

Karat. See CARAT/CARET/KARAT.

Key is not well used as a synonym of *essential*, *fundamental*, *most important*, or *indispensable*. Prefer any of these words, but choose the most appropriate. And avoid such sentences as "Ray is my *key* assistant," and "Our company plans to adopt a *key* policy soon."

Kind is a singular noun. Therefore, do not say, "*These kind* of onions *bite* my tongue," but "*This kind* of onion *bites* my tongue" or, in the best English, "Onions of *this kind* bite my tongue." Care must be exercised with the word *kind* not to mix singulars and plurals.

Avoid a superfluous *a* or *an*. Not "What kind of *a* coach is he?" but "What kind of coach is he?" And not "He deplores that kind of *an* investigation," but "that kind of investigation."

Using *kind of* as an adverb to represent *almost*, *rather*, or *somewhat* is colloquial. Prefer "He is *rather* heavy" to "*kind of* heavy" and "Arlene was *somewhat* surprised at the news" to "*kind of* surprised."

Sort follows the same conventions as *kind*. Say, "He was *somewhat* angry" instead of "*sort of* angry."

Knot is a nautical term representing speed. A ship may sail at seven knots. Adding *an hour*—"seven knots *an hour*"—is redundant. A knot is a unit of speed of one nautical mile an hour. It is not a measure of distance.

Known as. See HYPHENS.

L

Last is a superlative form of *late*. And so is *latest*. Although both mean "coming after all others," they have different applications. *Last*, in the sense of *final*, may refer to position ("the *last* boy in the row") or to time ("the *last* show of the night"). **Latest** implies not so much finality as *current* or *most recent*: "I know that my sister's *latest* boyfriend will not be her last." See FIRST.

Latter. See FORMER/LATTER.

Lay, meaning *to place*, is a *transitive verb*; that is, it takes an object: "I will *lay* the *books* [direct object] on your desk." **Lie**, meaning *to recline* or *to rest*, is *intransitive*. It takes no object: "I will *lie* down for an hour." (In this essay *to lie*, meaning *to tell a falsehood*, is not being considered.) Be careful of *lay*; it is both the present tense of the verb *lay* ("Leghorns *lay* large eggs"); it is also the past tense of the verb *lie* ("Andrew *lay* in the hammock all afternoon").

Note that *lie* has no form ending in *d*. This means that you should not say, "He *laid* down to take an early nap." Say, instead, "He *lay* down to take an early nap." *Laid*, as in "Albert *laid* the dishes on the first shelf," is the past tense of the transitive verb *lay*.

The principal parts of *lay* are *lay, laid, laid:* "Tom *lays* sod on Sundays"; "Tom *laid* sod last Sunday"; "Tom *has laid* sod for years." The principal parts of *lie* are *lie, lay, lain*: "The boys *lie* under a tree in the afternoon"; "The boys *lay* under a tree after lunch"; "The boys *have lain* under a tree every day this week."

Care must also be exercised to assure the proper use of the *-ing* forms of *lay* and *lie*. Do not confuse *laying* with *lying*. Not, "Perry spent the week *laying* on the beach," but "*lying* on the beach." And please note once more that the past participle of *lay* is *laid* (same as its past tense), whereas the past participle of *lie* is *lain*. Perhaps this essay should be reread, since *lie* and *lay* are among the most troublesome verbs in the English language.

Leave/let are frequently misused, each for the other. The answer to the question whether one should say, "*Leave* [or *let*] us go" depends on the level of usage. In standard English *let* means to permit or to allow; *leave* means to depart. Hence "*Let* us go" is correct. "*Leave* us go" is incorrect and unacceptable.

When *alone* accompanies *let* or *leave* in the sense of *not to disturb*, the words then are interchangeable: "When I'm studying please *leave* [or *let*] me *alone*."

Lend is a verb and **loan,** in formal language, is a noun: "The banks *lend* money"; "A person makes a *loan*." In business circles and in popular usage, *loan* is often used as a verb. But although saying, "The bank *loaned* Hy a thousand dollars," is acceptable, in other contexts prefer *lent*: "He *lent* his cousin a book on English synonyms."

Less. See FEWER.

Liable/likely/apt overlap in meaning to express *probability*. Although these words are often interchanged, prefer *apt* to mean *naturally inclined, having a known tendency toward* ("He's *apt* to jig when he hears music"), *likely* to mean that which is *expected* or *probable* ("The weather forecast says it is *likely* to rain today"), *liable* to mean the *probability of unpleasant consequences* ("A boy is *liable* to get run over if he darts out from between parked cars"). Prefer *likely* to *liable* in such sentences as "You're *liable* to see him playing tennis almost every Sunday," even though *liable* for *likely* is common.

An extra thought on *likely*. When used as an adverb meaning *probably*, idiom requires an escort: *most, quite, rather*, or *very*. Say, "Nora will *very likely* refuse to agree." "It is *most likely* going to snow before the day is over."

Libel/slander refer to *defamation*. Perhaps for that reason the words are often confused. *Libel* is defamation *by written or printed words, pictures, and so on*. *Slander* is defamation *by oral utterances*. This means that the same defamatory words may be libelous or slanderous, depending on how they have been publicized. It is wise to keep these legal distinctions clearly in mind.

Lie. See LAY.

Lighted/lit are interchangeable in all respects. You may say, properly, "She *lit* [or *lighted*] the Sabbath candles" and "My uncle *lighted* [or *lit*] his pipe." But idiom usually will lead you to one word or the other. We talk about a hallway's being "dimly *lighted*" but about a "well-*lit* vestibule." And we say, "The star's dressing room was well *lighted*, but unfortunately the stage was poorly *lit*."

Like/as are not interchangeable. *Like*, a preposition, introduces a comparison. It is the equivalent of *similar to* ("Asher is *like* his uncle"), or *in a manner similar to* ("If you act *like* your uncle, you'll be admired"), or *such as* ("English scholars *like* Edwin Newman are rare").

As, a conjuction, is the equivalent of *the way*, which can serve as a substitute: "If Ernie acts *as* [*the way*] it pleases him, he won't be invited anymore"; "My wife's spaghetti tastes good, *as* a pasta should." Note that—and here's a beacon—*as* introduces a group of words that contains a *verb*.

Be on guard not to misuse *like* for *as if* or *as though*. Instead of "He acted *like* he was the owner," say, "He acted *as if* [or *as though*] he *were* the owner." (When using *as if* or *as though*, which always introduces a statement that is not true, the subjunctive—in this case, *were*—is required.)

Likely. See LIABLE/LIKELY/APT.

Linking verbs, also called *copulative verbs* (*be, become, grow, look, smell, taste, turn,* and so on), link subject and predicate. A noun following a linking verb is called a *predicate noun*. Its function is to rename or explain the subject. For example, in

"Our math teacher is a fine golfer," *golfer*, while completing the meaning of the verb, refers to the subject. An adjective that completes the meaning of the verb is called a *predicate adjective*: "Our math teacher is *handsome*."

An important thing to remember is that linking verbs take either nouns or adjectives, but not adverbs as other verbs do. The reason is that these verbs serve merely as a link—"He is tall" in effect means "He *equals* tall." We therefore do not say, for example, "He feels *badly* [adverb] about his losses," since *feel* is a linking verb. We say, "He feels *bad* [adjective] about his losses." A person feels *badly* if his sense of touch is impaired or if he is wearing heavy gloves (here *feel* is an active verb). "My dog smells *bad*" means it needs a bath. With the active verb *smell* in "My dog smells *badly*," the sense is that something is wrong with its nose. Consider one more. In "He looked *hopefully* at the approaching ship," *looked* is an active verb. But in "He looks *well*" or in "He looks *exhausted*," *looks* is a linking verb, and the adjectives are joined to their subjects. See COPULATIVE VERBS; PREDICATE ADJECTIVES; PREDICATE NOMINATIVES; WELL.

Literally means *actually*, according to the strict definition of the word. It is incorrect to use *literally* as an intensifier, as in "Mr. Baxter was so angry he *literally* tore his hair out" unless he was thereby made bald. It is permissible, however, to say, "I literally threw the book at him; unfortunately it bounced off his left foot."

Lot/lots, meaning *much, a great deal of,* or *a great many,* are terms avoided by some discriminating speakers and writers in favor of one of the stated meanings. "We have *many* [not *lots of*] books on the English language in our library"; "Our hospital received *a great deal of* [not *lots of*] assistance from the community this year." But if *a lot* or *lots of* is used, be aware that the number of the verb is governed by the noun following *of*, not *a lot* or *lots*, the grammatical subject: "Lots of *food is* here"; "Lots of *hats have* arrived"; "A lot of *time has* been wasted"; "A lot of *employees have* reported in sick."

Note two things: *A lot* is being seen and heard more and more on all levels of usage and will soon be approaching the threshold of idiomatic acceptance. *A lot* is spelled as here, with two words— not *alot*. See SUBJECT OF A SENTENCE.

Luxuriant means *lush, flourishing, growing profusely*. **Luxurious** means *elegant, characterized by sumptuousness*. Therefore, do not say, "The castle we visited was *luxuriant*, and it was set in a garden of *luxurious* foliage." Switch the adjectives and correct the sentence.

-ly is a common adverb ending. A compound expression—that is, an adverb and participle or an adverb and adjective—in which the adverb ends in *-ly* should not be hyphenated. Not "It is a *brightly-lit* room" or "His was an *equally-good* plan." Omit the hyphens.

Remember that many adverbs do *not* end in *-ly*— *far, fast, little, often, soon, very, well*—whereas many adjectives do: *courtly, lively, lonely, lovely, manly, womanly*, just to cite a few. Care must therefore be taken to distinguish between adverbs and adjectives that end in -*ly*, because the adjectives *do* take hyphens in this position: "He is a *fatherly-looking* man"; "It was a *cowardly-sounding* defense."

Caution: Avoid the repetitive sound of two -*ly* words next to each other. Not "The coat buyer is *generally solely* responsible for buying cloth and fur coats." But "*Generally*, the coat buyer is *solely* responsible for buying cloth and fur coats." See AD-VERBS.

M

Majority/plurality are terms that most often apply to matters of voting. If two candidates are running for office, the one who receives more votes than the other has a *majority*. The candidate garnering the most votes, but no more than the combined votes of the other candidates, is said to have a **plurality.** If Tom received seventy votes, Ralph fifty, and Bill forty, Tom would have a *plurality* of twenty, but no majority. A plurality is *the difference in the count between the leader and the next highest candidate, there being no majority.*

Outside the field of voting, it is best to remember that the larger part of something should not be described as the *majority*. Rather than "A *majority* of the gravel was dumped early in the morning," say, "*Most* of the gravel." See COLLECTIVE NOUNS.

Manner is a term that can lead to wordiness. A sentence like "Milly did it *in a gracious manner*" is more economically put "Milly did it *graciously*." *In a stupid manner* needs only *stupidly*.

Many. See INDEFINITE PRONOUNS.

Many a/no/such a take singular verbs, even when introducing compound singular subjects, that is, subjects linked by *and*: "Such a show of affection *and* emotional response *was* unexpected"; "Many a writer *and* many a speaker *has* benefited from a study of my books"; "No man *and* no woman *is* permitted beyond these confines." See VERBS.

Masterful/masterly are words to be handled carefully. A *masterful* person is *domineering, strong-willed*. A *masterly* person is *skilled in his field. Masterly* might be used to describe the way a renowned orchestra leader conducts. This means that you should not refer to a "*masterful* performance." In fact, you will have little use for the word *masterful.*

May/might look to the future in that each word considers a possible happening. *May* connotes a greater likelihood than *might*, which makes *may* the stronger word. In "I *may* go," the probabilities are greater than in "I *might* go." *May* indicates a background of serious thought. "He *may* die" is more strongly put than "He *might* die." "He *may* succeed" sounds more hopeful than "He *might* succeed." *Might* expresses a greater degree of doubt and uncertainty.

Might is the past tense of *may*: "If Betty *had known* everything, she *might* not have gone," not "*may* not." But "If Betty now *knows* everything, she *may* not go," not *might* not. See CAN; MIXED TENSES.

Me. Whether to say, "It's *I*" or "It's *me*" is a disturbing matter because both forms have authoritative approval. "It is I" [or "It's I"] is formally correct. The classroom rule is that the verb *to be* takes the same case after it as before it. Hence nominative to nominative: "*It* is I." But many people, even some of the most educated, would say, "It's *me*" in everyday use, probably because it sounds more natural and less prissy than "It is I." See TO BE.

Meantime, usually a noun, and **meanwhile**, usually an adverb, are not interchangeable. "*In the meantime*, we will sing songs" is properly put, as is "*Meanwhile*, we will sing songs." But not "In the *meanwhile*, we will sing songs" or "*Meantime*, we will sing songs."

Measles. See SINGULAR AND PLURAL NOUNS.

Measurement, words of. See WEIGHTS.

Media is invariably plural. Therefore, not "The media *is* constantly blasting that candidate," but "The media *are*." Radio is a *medium* of communication; radio, television, and newspapers are *media*.

Meet/meet with mean *to encounter*, but each term is applied differently. In its ordinary sense *meet* means *to make the acquaintance of*; *meet with*, to *join company*. You *meet* your neighbor when he moves into his house; you *meet with* your neighbor to discuss common problems.

Memento means *souvenir*. *Momento* is simply a mispronunciation. Although Webster says that *momento* is a variant of *memento*, do not go along with that thinking.

Metaphors/similes are *figures of speech*. A metaphor *implies a similarity* or, to put it another way, *expresses an implied comparison*: "Bob is a lion";

"Jill is a doll"; "My brother is a tower of strength."
A simile *makes a comparison or indicates a similarity by using* like *or* as: "Bob is *like* a lion"; "Jill is *like* a doll."

Meticulous is a dangerous word to use because it has two unrelated senses, each one being in current usage. The meaning considered standard is *painstaking, scrupulous,* or *precise*: "Mary is a *meticulous* housekeeper"; "My secretary is *meticulous* in the handling of every assignment." But some people disregard this positive sense in favor of one less complimentary—*overcareful* or *fussy*: "My brother's *meticulous* cleaning of his car drives us all to distraction."

Might. See MAY.

Might perhaps is a redundancy, since each word suggests a possibility. Use one or the other.

Militate/mitigate are confusable words. Things that *militate against* a person's success are those that work against him. The key to the correct use of *militate* is the preposition *against,* since *against* always follows *militate.* To *mitigate* means *to lessen, moderate,* or *make less severe,* as might be the case in a milder sentence rendered by a court of justice. Remember that the combination *mitigate against* does not exist.

Mixed tenses weaken writing. They are distracting. Not "I should be so pleased if you *will* come tonight," but "I *should* be pleased if you *would* come tonight" or "I *shall* be pleased if you *will* come tonight."

Convention calls for *could, would, should,* or *might* after a verb in the past tense: "The dean *declared* that the school *might* [not *may*] close for renovations." Otherwise, in the present, present perfect, and future tenses, use *can, will, shall,* or *may.*

Money. See WEIGHTS/MONEY/MEASUREMENTS.

Momentarily is ambiguous when used with the future tense. It may mean either *for a moment* or *in a moment.* Therefore, instead of "My aunt will be here *momentarily,*" say, "My aunt's visit will *be brief*" or "My aunt will *come soon*"—and be understood.

Momentarily, strangely, in both the present and past tense means only "for a moment," which is a short while.

A word with a similar problem is **presently.** It also has two senses: *now* and *soon.* "Come in. The doctor will see you *presently*" (*now*). "Have a seat. The doctor will see you *presently*" (*soon*).

Mood is a term in grammar that does not have to be a part of the vocabulary of speakers and writers. As a practical matter, only the functioning of the subjunctive mood need be known, and that mood is largely moribund, now restricted by users to only a few applications.

The following is set out for those who wish an overall picture of the three English moods. In any event, some useful information might be gleaned by almost anyone.

Mood is *the manner in which a verb is used.* It is the grammatical way of expressing an attitude toward the assertion one makes. A statement of

fact ("It is now four o'clock") or a question con-
cerning fact ("What time did you say it was?") is
in the *indicative mood*. The *subjunctive mood* (*be*,
were) expresses a wish, a desire ("I wish I *were*
going") or an improbable condition, one that is contrary to fact ("If I *were* President, I would act differently"). The *imperative mood* expresses simple
commands ("*Stop!*") or requests ("Please *be* careful
of our flowers").

A simple condition is in the indicative mood ("If
I *was* not there, I must have been out of town"; "If
I *was* careless, I'm sorry"). In these last two exam-
ples the *if* clause does not say whether it is true.

Moose. See SINGULAR AND PLURAL SUBJECTS.

More. See INDEFINITE PRONOUNS.

More than one, when followed by a singular noun
or pronoun as subject, takes a singular verb ("More
than one exercise *has* been proposed"), even though
the phrase suggests several (that is, *more than one*).

If words intervene between *more* and *than one*, then
you must use a plural verb: "More politicians than one
have been charged with bribery in this town."

Most is not an equivalent of *almost* (not "*Most*
everyone was there," but *almost everyone*). When
wondering whether to use *most* or *almost* in a sentence, try *almost* first. If it works, it is the word to
use. Note that *almost* means *nearly*: *almost*
(nearly) everyone, *almost* (nearly) everywhere. *Most*
is also not an equivalent of *very*—not "He was
most kind," but *very kind*.

As an adjective, *most* means *nearly all* ("*Most*

politicians make their living by talking"). As an adverb *most* indicates the superlative degree of adjectives (*most beautiful*) and adverbs (*most loudly*). As a pronoun, meaning *the largest part of, most*, although the grammatical subject, is a singular or a plural depending on the number of the noun in the *of* phrase: "Most of the *dogs* here *are* poodles"; "Most of the *lawn is* brown." See INDEFINITE PRONOUNS.

Much. See PAST PARTICIPLES.

Must. See BUT WHAT.

Must of. See OF.

Mutual is a word that should be used to mean *something reciprocated by two or more persons.* The thing to remember is that the sense of *mutual* is "reciprocal." If you and I like each other, we have a *mutual* friendship. If a husband and wife are affectionate toward each other, they enjoy *mutual* affection. *Mutual* refers to the relationship of people to each other or to one another.

Common refers to *things shared equally*, such as a common cause, a common enemy, or a common interest. If both you and I like Byron, we share a *common* admiration. If we both like tennis, we have a common interest. *Common* refers to people's relationship to something other than their feelings toward each other.

An exception to what has just been said is the phrase *mutal friend.* The friend is really *a friend in common.* But *mutual friend* is such a long-standing phrase, and in such common use, that with few exceptions it is accepted by all usage authorities.

N

Name. See CONSIDER.

Named. See HYPHENS.

Namely. See THAT IS.

Nauseous means *causing or affected by nausea, sickening, disgusting* ("a *nauseous* sight"). **Nauseated** means *experiencing nausea* (a *nauseated* airplane passenger"). Just as one is scandalized by something scandalous, so one is nauseated by something nauseous. If a person were nauseous, he would make other people sick.

The fact is that many people, even educated people, use *nauseous* mistakenly for *nauseated*. A person with a queasy stomach is nauseated. A passenger aboard a ship who feels her stomach revolting is nauseated, not nauseous. In good contexts the distinction between these words is maintained.

Ad nauseam, "to the point of nausea," should be spelled as given, not as so commonly seen: *ad nauseum.*

Near future/the not too distant future are not precise terms. But the expressions have become established in everyday speech because everyone understands what the speaker means. Of course, using *soon* for the first and *eventually* for the second is more in keeping with better English, even though those terms do not pinpoint the time either.

Another "future" expression, *foreseeable future*, is regarded as acceptable idiom. Although imprecise, it is understandable—and useful. No one would, in ordinary conversation, take the expression to refer to a time fifty years away. The clear intent is to refer to the expected immediate period that one might reasonably consider.

Needless to say is regarded by some critics as an undesirable phrase, the argument being that if it is needless, why say it? Their thinking has merit. Nevertheless, the phrase serves the useful purpose of calling attention to a thought about to be expressed. Feel free (but only occasionally) to use it. The critics also object to the phrase *it goes without saying* on the ground that if that is so, it should not be said. Regardless, experience has shown that the expression is sometimes a useful device. And that goes without saying.

Negative subject—when joined to a positive subject—does not govern the number of the verb. The positive does: "It is Evelyn, not her parents, who *is* expected." "It is the parents, not Evelyn, who *are* expected."

Neither/nor. See EITHER/OR, NEITHER/NOR; INDEFINITE PRONOUNS; CORRELATIVE CONJUNCTIONS.

Never is not a satisfactory replacement for *not*. *Never* means *at no time* or *not ever*. Therefore, instead of saying, "That man never told me who he was," say, "That man did *not* tell me who he was." And not "Jack never came this morning," but "Jack did *not* come this morning." It is correct to say, however, "My mother has *never* visited Japan."

Nevertheless. See BUT.

News. See SINGULAR AND PLURAL NOUNS.

Nice. See ADJECTIVES.

No. Two or more singular subjects modified by *no*, although connected by *and*, take a singular verb: "*No* boy under fourteen *and no* girl under sixteen *is* to be admitted without accompanying parents." See MANY A; INDEFINITE PRONOUNS.

Nominative absolute is an expression you may run into. You needn't know much about it. But you should know that it exists and that it is not connected grammatically to the rest of the sentence. It is somewhat of an outlaw construction but is regarded as correct English. An example is, "*The sun having risen,* we set out for the hills." The first expression—"The sun having risen"—is a participal phrase grammatically unrelated to any other word in the sentence. Take another: "*The rain being intolerable,* I decided to stay at home." The phrase does not modify *I*, the subject of the sentence, or *home*, the object of the preposition *at*.

None calls for a singular verb if the meaning is *not one*: "None of the three plays I saw this season *was* worth seeing"; "None of the apples she gave us *was* edible." But *none* becomes a plural if its meaning is *not any*: "None of the clothes on display at the museum *were* of Victorian style"; "None of the trees in the rear lawn *have* been pruned." *None* is logically singular, but it is often regarded as a plural. See INDEFINITE PRONOUNS.

Nonrestrictive clauses. See RESTRICTIVE/NONRESTRICTIVE CLAUSES.

Noplace. See ANYPLACE.

Nor is used either to correlate with *neither* (*neither . . . nor*) or to follow a negative statement (one containing *no* or *not*) that does not carry through to a second clause, as in "We will *not* go, *nor* will we donate anything." *Or* is used after a negative if what follows merely adds or amplifies: "I do *not* have a fishing hook, *or* even a minnow."

Some writers use *nor* in still another way—to add distinctiveness and emphasis to an expression following a negative. They point out that, say, "Harry has no money or assets of any kind" is not so emphatic as, "Harry has no money *nor* assets of any kind." The style to be used here is a personal matter between the writer and his pen. See CONJUNCTIONS.

Not. See NEVER.

Not all is an expression that can lead to ambiguity. Consider "All children are not afraid of dogs." That is obviously untrue. Change the position of *not* to make the example accurate: "*Not all* children are afraid of dogs." Take another: "All that is appealing is not necessarily good" should be reworded, "*Not all* that is appealing is necessarily good." But note Shakespeare's "All that glitters [really *glisters*] is not gold." It would have read more accurately had *not* begun the sentence. Nevertheless, the expression is now idiomatic.

Not only is usually followed by *but also*—"We will be visiting *not only* the Grossmans *but also* the Shupaks"—and never by *as well as* (not "*Not only* Arlene *as well as* Joanne will be there"). As a matter of writing style, *also* may be omitted to intensify what follows: "Mac is *not only* the brightest boy in his class, *but* [no *also*] the brightest boy in the entire school."

When using this correlative conjunction, observe structural balance, that is, make the phrasing after *not only* the same structure as that after *but also*. If a noun or a preposition follows the one, use a noun or a preposition, or whatever the case may be, after *but also*. "Dan is not only *rich* [adjective] but also *handsome* [adjective]" and not "Dan not only *is* rich but also handsome." Change "Not only boys are invited but also girls" to "Not only boys but also girls are invited."

A writing tip: Use *and* instead of *not only/but also* where emphasis is not required. For example, "He was not only handsome but also wealthy" would read more economically as "He was handsome *and* wealthy." See CORRELATIVE CONJUNCTIONS.

Noun—the name of a *person, place, thing,* or *quality.* Or in more concise form: A *noun* is the *name of an object or idea.* The two categories of nouns are *proper*—the official name for a person, an object, or a group, such as New York, Pacific, Nebraska, Thomas—and *common*—such as tree, chair, child, building. In sum, the noun is *the naming word*. See COLLECTIVE NOUNS.

Nowhere/noplace. See ANYPLACE.

Nowheres. See ANYPLACE.

Number in grammar is a word form that shows whether the word is singular or plural. It applies to nouns (*boy* and *ox* are singular, *boys* and *oxen* are plural); pronouns (*he, she, it* are singular, *we* and *they* are plural); and verbs ("The *girl* goes" is singular and "The *girls* go" is plural).

As a collective noun, *number* may be treated as a singular or a plural word, depending on whether it is preceded by *the* or *a*: "*The number* of barrels still unsold *is* disappointing"; "*A number* of barrels we've recently received *are* broken." Observe that *the number* takes a singular verb and that *a number* takes a plural verb. See AMOUNT.

Number given to nouns. See SINGULAR AND PLURAL NOUNS.

Numbers are best spelled out if less than one hundred ("My grammar school teacher is *ninety-seven* years old") and expressed in figures if above a hundred ("There are *104* students in our class").

If two numbers follow each other, spell out the shorter word: "Please send me 75 ten-cent stamps." The ordinal numbers for street designations (*3rd, 15th*) are becoming old-fashioned. Prefer cardinal numbers: "I live at 1809 S. 6 Street."

The general rule is to spell out numbers that can be expressed in one or two words: *ten; sixty-seven.* Also, spell out large round numbers: "Fifteen hundred people were there." In that example, *fifteen hundred* would have to be spelled out anyway, since figures should never begin a sentence.

O

Objective complement—a grammatical term that one need not know in order to speak or write good English. It is included here for those who wish to know how it functions.

This complement is a noun or adjective that follows the direct object to complete its meaning by explaining or describing it: "The club elected *Albert* [direct object] *president* [objective complement]." "We dug the *hole* [direct object] *deep* [objective complement]." To test for an objective complement, mentally place *to be* after the direct object; for example, "... Albert *to be* president," "... hole *to be* deep."

Observance/observation are not to be misused, one for the other. The first is *the act or practice of complying with a law, custom, command, or other prescribed duty.* "City Hall is closed today in *observance* of Veterans' Day." *Observation* is *paying attention* or *noticing.* We speak of one's powers of observation and the strict observance of laws, rituals, and duties.

Obviously. See ADVERBS.

Oculist/ophthalmologist/optometrist/optician are persons trained to care for their patients' eyes. The first two terms are synonyms. A physician who specializes in diseases of the eye may be called an *oculist* or an *ophthalmologist,* the latter being the term preferred by the medical profession. An *optometrist* has been trained to measure the range of vision and prescribe corrective lenses. An *optician* is a person trained to make eyeglasses and other optical goods.

Of should not replace *have* after *could, might, must,* or *should:* "I *could have* done it if asked," not "I *could of*"; and not "We *should of* left earlier," but "We *should have.*" Likewise, avoid the combination *had of,* as in "If Robert *had of* known, he would have bought it today." Say, "If Robert *had* known, he would have bought it today" (no *of*).

Off of. See DOUBLE PREPOSITIONS.

"Of" phrases. See SUBJECT OF SENTENCE.

Omission of words, properly and improperly. When *that* is not the object of a verb, it may be omitted (except in formal writing): "I was so exhausted [no *that*] I could hardly stand up." This bypassing also applies to *whom,* when its omission does not affect the sense of the sentence—"We liked the last applicant [no *whom*] we interviewed"—or when a final preposition is anticipated: "Agnes is the woman [no *whom*] we gave it *to.*"

In "When going on a hike, be sure to wear sturdy shoes," the omitted "you are" ("When *you are* going . . .") is easily supplied, and therefore properly omitted, as is true of the implied *has been* before *bathed* in "The dog has been found and bathed already."

Addendum: A verb in a clause need not be repeated in a subsequent clause if its omission causes no confusion. A comma may serve instead: "His short story was bad; his novel, even worse."

Caveat: Do not omit any form of a verb combination. "Bessie always has and always will be prompt" should be restated: "Bessie always has *been* and always will be prompt." See AS; COMPARATIVE FORMS OF ADJECTIVES; ELLIPSIS; SUPERLATIVE FORMS; THE.

On/onto/on to serve different functions. The preposition *on* indicates *a position of rest* (*on* the sofa) or *time when* (*on* August 18) or *continued motion* (worked *on* through the night). The preposition *onto* means *to a position on* ("Barney ran *onto* the field"; "Hiram leaped *onto* the counter"). In *on to* (two words), *on* is an adverb that is a part of the verb (a phrasal verb)—*went on, traveled on*—and *to* is a preposition: "Fred went *on to* more important assignments"; "Amos traveled *on to* Chicago."

On behalf of. See BEHALF.

One as an impersonal pronoun referring to an average person, unfortunately, is not problem-free. Whether to repeat *one* ("*One* has a right to *one's* own lifestyle") or to switch to the possessive pronouns ("*One* has a right to *his* [or to *his or her*] own lifestyle") has proponents on both sides. To many users *one* sounds wooden, and when used in a series, awkward and monotonous. Many writers would use *he*: "When *one* enters a room, *he* should remove his hat." This style of writing is smoother, more natural, and is the way English has been written almost from its birth. The change of pronouns, although a violation of the rule of consistency, is, as so used, permissible—and advisable.

Where a plural pronoun could serve without distorting the meaning of the sentence, it would not only relieve the problem but also counteract a charge of offensive sexism.

One another. See EACH OTHER/ONE ANOTHER.

One of the/one of those who are expressions that take a plural verb, despite the preceding singular *one*. In "Al is *one of the men* who live [not *lives*] on our street" and in "Pauline is *one of those people who* are [not *is*] always arguing," a plural verb is required because *who* refers to plural *men/people*, not to *one*. To prove the point, invert the sentence: "Of the *men* who *live* on our street, Al is one" and "Of those *people* who *are* always arguing, Pauline is one."

The grammatical community has been in a turmoil about this construction, since some critics think that the singular *one* should govern. But by far, most grammarians hold that the plural is strictly correct.

Note, however, that the combination *only one* calls for a singular verb: "Bob is the *only one* of the students who *is* sure to receive a scholarship." Respect the singularity of *only* in this kind of phrasing.

One or more is a plural expression. Bernstein points out that "Inside each folder is one or more sheets of information" should be reworded, "*are one or more*." See MORE THAN ONE, which is oppositely constructed.

Only is very possibly the most frequently misplaced adverb. Like other modifiers, *only* should be placed as close as possible to the word or words it modifies. In this way the intended meaning is precisely conveyed. The sentence "Jackson *only had* ten dollars with him at the time of his arrest" does not confuse anyone, but in better writing, *only* should be properly positioned, next to the words it modifies. Note that the change involves the repositioning of *only* from before the verb to after it ("had *only* ten dollars"). In "Darwin *only* developed the theory of evolution after many years of thought and research," the indication is that the theory was all that Darwin did. Since this of course is not the case, *only* should precede *after:* "*only* after many years of thought and research." See ADVERBS.

Onto. See ON, ONTO, ON TO.

Onward/onwards. See TOWARD/TOWARDS.

Ophthalmologist. See OCULIST.

Optician. See OCULIST.

Optometrist. See OCULIST.

Or. See CONJUNCTIONS; EITHER/OR, NEITHER/NOR; NOR.

Oral/verbal are words that do not confuse many people, although *verbal* is frequently used imprecisely. *Oral* pertains to the mouth: *oral* surgeon. It therefore, in this context, means *expressed in speech.* An oral contract is an agreement made through spoken words.

Verbal is the culprit here because it means *pertaining to words*, which does not limit its sense to unwritten words. That which is *verbal* may be spoken *or* written. Nevertheless, in everyday language *verbal* is regarded as the equivalent of *oral*. Confusing? It may be in some instances. It is therefore preferable, and advisable, to use *oral* to mean spoken, and to use *written* to mean that which has been reduced to writing. The use of *verbal* should perhaps be restricted to comparison of matters of words, signs, and symbols, but not of utterances.

Note the word *aural*, which sounds like *oral*. *Aural* means *received through the ear*, which is the way an *oral* message is received.

Ordinal numbers. See FIRST, SECOND, THIRD.

Ordinance/ordnance are words whose meanings are unrelated. An *ordinance* is a local law. In a fuller sense, it is a rule, law, decree, or regulation. *Ordnance* is military equipment.

Other *four* or *four others* (or whatever number is used) are not interchangeable. In fact, they are sometimes confused, with ludicrous results.

In the sentence "On the first ballot three jurors voted to acquit but the other nine voted to convict," a recast is required: "the nine *others* voted to convict." Saying "the *other nine*" implies a previous nine.

Others. See INDEFINITE PRONOUNS.

Otherwise. See COMPARATIVE FORMS.

Outside of. See ACCEPT/EXCEPT; DOUBLE PREPOSITIONS.

Over is accepted on all levels of English to mean *more than*. One may properly say, "There were *over* twenty people there." But this is not to say that *more than* is not preferable. It is.

Over with. See DOUBLE PREPOSITIONS.

P

Parallelism. See EITHER/OR, NEITHER/NOR.

Pants. See SINGULAR AND PLURAL NOUNS.

Parameter is a vogue word, usually used to impress. It should be employed with discretion, and only by those who understand what it means. And they are very few. *Parameter* is a mathematical term meaning a *constant*, the value of which can vary according to how it is applied. Is there much need for that word in general writing? You answer that one.

Those who use *parameter* instead of perimeter, limit, or boundary probably do so in the belief that they are sounding more important and more impressive to their audience. The suggestion here is not to use this word. In fact, any writing that sounds high-blown should be avoided.

Parenthetical elements are words that have no effect on the number of the subject. In "Fred, as well as his brother, are to enter Dartmouth," change *are* to *is*, since Fred is a singular subject and the *as well as* phrase is parenthetical. Likewise, in "Johnson, *together with* [or *accompanied by*] three engineers, are surveying the building," here too change *are* to *is*, and for the same reasons. And so we say, "Sclafani, *along with* two of his friends, *was* jailed for contempt." See AS WELL AS; INTERVENING WORDS.

Partake—a person is sometimes said to *partake* of refreshments—is such a stilted and old-fashioned word that it is best forgotten. It is preferable to say, "Let's eat," or "Let's have a meal together," than to use *partake*. And remember that *partake* is not a synonym of *participate*, which means *to engage in some activity.*

Partial is a two-headed word. It means both *incomplete* (a *partial* review) and *prejudiced* (*partial* to his cousin's ideas). A sentence out of context, such as "It was a *partial* survey," does not tell us whether the survey was *incomplete* or *biased*.

The adverb *partially* may also be a semantic trap. Consider "The minutes were *partially* recorded." It may mean *taking one side* or *not totally*. Here you may try *partly*.

Participle—a verb form that is used as an adjective. The present participle ends in -*ing*. In "We heard him singing," *singing* is a participle modifying *him*. The past participle has many endings, most frequently -*ed*. In "The general coughed while being photographed," *being photographed* modifies *general*. In "Having finished the job, Tony called for the truck," *having finished* modifies Tony.

Note the difference in function between a present participle and a GERUND (both end in -*ing*). In "The coach saw Fred running," *running* is a participle modifying Fred. In "The coach timed Fred's running," *running* is a gerund, or verbal noun. The coach was recording Fred's speed. See GERUNDS; PAST PARTICIPLES.

Parts of speech is a technical term you can function without. But it is well to know that the term exists, for you may read it somewhere. The *parts of speech* are the eight groups of words that comprise all the words in the English language: nouns, pronouns, verbs, adjectives, adverbs, prepositions, conjunctions, and interjections. These parts of speech are discussed separately in this book.

Passive voice. See VOICE.

Past participles are treated like adjectives ("a *frightened* rabbit"). The unresolved, or partly resolved, problem involving these participles is the proper use of *very* to modify them. The test most often applied is whether the participle has become a true adjective. If yes, it may be modified by *very* ("Amy is *very pleased*"). If no, you must use *much* or *very much* ("the plan is *much* [or *very much*] improved").

Judging whether a past participle is now being used as an unadulterated adjective is a difficult matter, and a controversial one. See TOO; VERY.

Past perfect tense indicates that an earlier action occurred before a later one or, to state it differently, it indicates past action as completed before some other past action. For example, "Mary *returned* the dress that she *had bought*"; "Jim *was upset* because he *had* not *been invited*."

Note that this tense is formed with *had* and a past participle. You might say that *had* is the sign of the past perfect tense.

One caution: When either *before* or *after* is used, or a dependent clause itself indicates a preceding time, the past perfect tense is thereby made unnecessary. In fact, its use would be redundant. With time indicated, the past tense should serve: "Jules *finished* the job before I arrived"; "Thomas reported that his uncle *said* last night that he would buy the old house." Not *had finished*, not *had said*.

Pay. See INDIRECT OBJECTS.

People is a word best used to designate a large, uncounted group ("About five thousand *people* attended") or an anonymous group ("Lincoln was a man of the *people*"). *Persons* should be used when specifying a small or exact number: "Four *persons* were in the room"; "We counted 107 *persons*." Bernstein's argument as to why *persons* must be used of an exact number has convinced many usage critics to support his thinking. He says, "If three people were in a room and two left, how many people would still be there? One people?" That of course makes no sense. Switching *people* to *persons* gives us a sensible—and correct—answer: *one person.* See INDIVIDUAL PERSON.

Per should not be substituted for *a* except in technical writing. Say, "He earned six dollars *a day*," not *per day*. But if avoiding *per* for *a* makes a statement clumsy, choose *per*. Prefer "Serve one ounce of salad *per* person" and "The writing expected of each man *per* year is governed by a set formula." Naturally if Latin phrases are called for, *per* is properly used at all times: *per annum, per diem.*

Percent/percentage should be distinguished. If attendance goes up from ten percent to twenty percent, the increase was ten *percentage* points but one hundred *percent.* Spell *percent* solid, as here.

Persecute/prosecute are sometimes mixed up, possibly because someone who is being prosecuted thinks he's being persecuted. To *persecute* is *to plague, to bring suffering to.* To *prosecute* is *to bring court action against.*

Period of time, in the opinion of some critics, is a redundancy because *time* is inherent in the word *period.* The suggestion here is not to use the phrase where either *period* ("a long *period*") or *time* ("a long *time*") will do.

Permanent truths. See GENERAL TRUTHS.

Person, in grammar, is defined as "the change in pronouns and verbs to show the person speaking (first person), or the person spoken to (second person), or the person or thing spoken of (third person)." The first person uses *I* or *we;* the second, *you;* and the third, *he, she, it,* or *they.*

Persons. See PEOPLE.

Persuade. See CONVINCE.

Phrase—in grammar, *a group of words that lacks a subject and a predicate;* for example, *the fat lady, covered by clouds, a rainy afternoon.* Many phrases consist of only two or three associated words: *according to, as well as.* See PREDICATE.

"—place" words. See ANYPLACE.

Placement of words. See ADVERBS; ADJECTIVE PHRASES.

Pleaded. See PLED/PLEADED.

Pled/pleaded are past tenses of *plead.* Conservative writers accept only *pleaded*, arguing that *pled* is dialectal. The conservatives, however, are fighting a losing battle. *Pled* is used more and more: "The defendant *pled* guilty."

Plenty is used correctly in "I've got *plenty* of nuthin." But not in "I've got *plenty corn* to be cut." An *of* must come between *plenty* and *corn.* In fact, *of* must always be used between *plenty* and a following noun. Furthermore, you may not use it as a qualifier: "I am *plenty* annoyed"; "He is *plenty* rich." You might say, instead, "He is *very* [or *extremely* or *quite*] rich." See VERY.

Pliers. See SINGULAR AND PLURAL NOUNS.

Plurality. See MAJORITY.

Plural nouns. See SINGULAR NOUNS.

Plus is not a conjunction. It is a preposition, the equivalent of *with.* Therefore, "The boy *plus* his gear *weighs* 150 pounds," not *weigh.* Just as we say, "Six minus two *is* four," so we say, "Four *plus* [meaning *with the addition of*] two *is* six" (not *are*). But bear in mind that "two and two *are* four" because *and* is a conjunction.

Since *plus* is a preposition, a phrase introduced by it does not affect the number of the verb: "The rock star plus his full entourage *is* now entering the fair grounds." The supplementary information headed by *plus* may be surrounded by commas: "The rock star, plus his entire entourage, is now entering the fair grounds."

In informal writing *plus* is used to mean *besides* or *in addition* ("The department has three editors, *plus* two secretaries and an indexer"). Many writers deplore this informal usage.

P.M. See A.M.

Politics. See SINGULAR AND PLURAL NOUNS.

Positive and negative subjects. See NEGATIVE AND POSITIVE SUBJECTS.

Possess should not displace the ordinary verb *have* or *own*, when the sense is mere ownership ("He *has* [not *possesses*] three cars and two trucks"), for in that usage *possess* is considered stilted. But this is not to say that in some contexts *possess* should not be used. For example, it is properly used in "In your patience *possess* ye your souls," and "Talent is what a man *possesses*; genius is what *possesses* a man."

Possessives, and the way they are shown, are governed by this basic rule: Use only of people, animals, and other forms possessing life. Therefore, not "The red roof's chimney needs repair," but "The *chimney on the red roof* needs repair." Exceptions are made of expressions denoting time, space, or measure ("a *week's* vacation," "an *hour's* time," "a *dollar's* worth," "the *day's* end").

Possessive singular nouns are generally formed by adding *'s* ("a *man's* privilege," "the *ox's* tail," "a *hostess's* time," "Bill *Thomas's* boat"). Plural nouns ending in *s* need only an apostrophe ("the *ladies'* coats," "the *Penicos'* hideaway"), but *'s* for plural nouns not ending in *s*: "the *men's* room," "the *children's* books," "the *people's* whims." Some stylists prefer only an apostrophe after a singular noun ending in *s*: "*Charles'* coat."

Possessive pronouns do not take apostrophes. Not "The books are Cecilia's and the pens are her's too." Change *her's* to *hers*. Indefinite pronouns are excepted: "*Someone's* umbrella was left behind." But note "*Her* and *his* books," not "*Hers* and *his* books." And do not be misled into thinking that *it's* is a possessive form. It isn't. It is a contraction of *it is*.

Compounds of possessive nouns are made by adding an apostrophe and *s* to the last element: "the attorney *general's* code of ethics," "the editor in *chief's* policies." Their plural form is constructed by pluralizing the main word: "the *sisters*-in-law's houses," not "the sister-in-laws' houses." A sign identifying a family residence should be in the possessive plural: "The *Smiths'* House," not "The *Smith's* House," a common mistake. And instead of "The *Browne's* live here," make it "The *Brownes* live here." No possessive is called for. See ITS; DOUBLE POSSESSIVE.

Possible . . . may is a redundant construction in such a sentence as "It is *possible* that the President *may* name him Secretary of State." Make it either

"It is *possible* that the President *will* name him Secretary of State" (no *may*) or "The President *may* name him Secretary of State" (no *possible*).

Pour/spill are synonymous terms, but their uses differ. To *pour* is to direct the flow of a liquid carefully. To *spill* is to allow the liquid to run haphazardly without particular attention to where it runs.

Practicable. See PRACTICAL.

Practical seems like an easy word not to misuse. But unfortunately, it is sometimes confused with its cousin **practicable**. *Practical,* when applied to persons, means *realistic, sensible*. When it relates to acts or processes, it means *workable, manageable,* or *useful. Practicable* means *capable of being accomplished, feasible,* or *possible*. We must be aware of the fact that something practicable may not necessarily be practical; that is, although it could be done or accomplished, it might be too costly or dangerous. It would then not be considered practical.

Practicable applies only to things; *practical* applies both to things and to persons.

Practically in everyday conversation means *almost* or *nearly* ("We are *practically* there"). But in precise usage it means *in practical terms* or *for practical purposes*. It is therefore, in the opinion of careful writers, not a synonym of *almost, as good as,* or *virtually*. "With only five dollars left, we are *virtually* [*almost, as good as, in effect*] out of money," not "*practically* out of money."

Predicate—*the part of a sentence that makes a statement about the subject.* The predicate consists of everything in the sentence except the subject—the verb, its complements, and its modifiers: "The girl [subject] *on the stage is my youngest sister*" [predicate]. The predicate is the moving part of the sentence. It tells what is doing or what is happening to the subject.

Predicate adjective—an adjective that follows a LINKING VERB, such verbs as *appear, be, feel, grow, keep, look, prove, remain, seem, sound,* and *stay*: "Our neighbor is *efficient*"; "The roast smells *good*." Both *efficient* and *good* are adjectives.

Whereas modifiers of action verbs are adverbs, those of linking verbs are always adjectives. Here are some examples in contrast: "The oven works *well*" (adverb); "The cake stayed *fresh*" (adjective). "She stared *coldly*" (adverb), but "She looks *cold*" (adjective). "He speaks *candidly*" (adverb), but "He seems *tired*" (adjective). One more: "The people *grew wild* when they learned that war had been declared." Here *grew* (linking verb) and *wild* (adjective) mean that the people *were* or *became* wild. In "The daisies *grew wildly* after the storm," the daisies were actually blooming in profusion. See LINKING VERBS; SUBJECT OF A SENTENCE; VERBS; WELL.

Predicate nominatives are *nouns or pronouns that follow the linking verb* "to be." They rename the subject and are, of course, in the nominative case. Therefore, not "If I were him, I would have left earlier," but "If I were *he*." And not "Sally? It may be her, although I doubt it," but "Sally? It may be *she*." See LINKING VERBS; PREDICATE ADJECTIVES; TO BE.

Prefer may be followed by *to* or *over*, but not by *than*. We say, "I *prefer* blueberries *to* raspberries" or "blueberries *over* raspberries," but not "I *prefer* blueberries *than* raspberries."

The only serious problem with *prefer* occurs when an infinitive follows it. You can't very well say, "I prefer to eat blueberries *to to* eat raspberries." One way out of this *to to* morass is to rephrase and say, "I prefer to eat blueberries *rather than* to eat raspberries." Of course you might say, "I prefer eating blueberries to raspberries" or use some other phrasing, but that is not answering the *to to* question.

Premises. See SINGULAR AND PLURAL NOUNS.

Preposition—the part of speech that *shows the relation between certain words*. The major word following a preposition is called its *object* and is always in the objective case. This point applies primarily to pronouns because they change forms from nominative to objective. In "The boy jumped *from the bridge*," *bridge* is the object of *from*, but since *bridge* is a noun, its form does not change when used as a nominative: "The *bridge* is long." However, although we say, "*She and I* will leave to buy a book," we say, "The book is *for her and me*." See BETWEEN.

Prepositions at the end of a sentence should be examined carefully, especially in formal writing, because important words and ideas, sometimes placed first in the sentence, are more often placed last, the last position being the most emphatic. This means that ordinarily a preposition, a weak word, should not end a sentence. But when idiom or rhythm demands that a preposition end a sentence, one should write accordingly. Certainly, the following example is smoother and preferable with the preposition at the end: "He is the boy my son plays with" rather than "He is the boy with whom my son plays." And so with "We had nothing to talk about" rather than "We had nothing about which to talk" or "It is a matter we often thought of" rather than "It is a matter of which we often thought." The prepositions *about* and *of* sound natural where placed. If we move them, we wind up with a clumsy locution.

Remember the mocking retort of Winston Churchill when chided for ending a sentence with a preposition: "This is the type of arrant pedantry up with which I shall not put." See AT; BETWEEN.

Present perfect tense—the tense used *to express action begun in the past and continuing into the present time*: "This *has been* a humid spring"; "I *have lived* in Florida for five years." Some grammarians say that the past tense is used for finished business ("John *did* not *come* home last night") and the present perfect tense for unfinished business ("John *has* not *come* home yet"). You would not say, "John *did* not *come* home yet." Or consider another: "Scott *has been* an accountant for twelve years" tells us that Scott is still practicing accounting. "Scott *was* an accountant for twelve years" tells us that Scott is no longer practicing his profession.

One more feature. The present perfect tense is also used *to express an action completed in the recent indefinite past.* Concededly, the past tense must be used if the time of the action is definitely given, as in "Ralph *went* home early today." But this is not so in "Mom *has baked* the cake already." The time here is indefinite; hence the present perfect tense.

Presently. See MOMENTARILY.

Principal, meaning *chief* or *main,* is both an adjective (*principal* committees, *principal* factors) and a noun, meaning the *head* or *leader,* the *employer of an agent,* or *invested capital:* "Mr. Lilly is the *principal* of our school." "An agent binds his *principal*"; "The loan, including *principal* and interest, came to $450". **Principle,** a noun only, refers to a fundamental or general truth: "The *principle* we live by is that honesty is the best policy"; "We will fight for our *principles.*" It is often used to mean a rule of conduct or a standard of judgment.

A helpful hint, to spell these words correctly, is to remember that *rule* ends in *le* and that *principle,* which is a rule, also ends in *le.*

Principal parts of a verb is an expression that may not seem important in everyday use. But if you know the principal parts of a verb—the present tense, the past tense, and the past participle—you'll have no trouble forming any tense of that verb.

Present tense: *I love*; past tense: *I loved*; past participle: *I have loved.* Present tense: *I call*; past tense: *I called*; past participle: *I have called.*

Principle. See PRINCIPAL.

Pronoun—the part of speech that is *a substitute for a noun.* The *pro* in *pronoun* means *for.* Pronouns reduce the monotony that a repetition of nouns would cause. We therefore replace the noun with a pronoun. Instead of saying, "David went to David's closet to look for David's tennis racquet," we say, "David went to *his* closet to look for *his* tennis racquet."

Pronouns that refer to a noun must agree with the noun in *gender* (masculine or feminine), *number* (singular or plural), and *person* (almost all are in the third person—*he, she, it, they*). The grammatical name for the noun is the *antecedent*. In "The boy is going to *his* house" and in "Everyone wore *her* hair in a bun," *boy* and *everyone* are the antecedents of *his* and *her*.

Be particularly careful of the proper number to give a pronoun that refers to a COLLECTIVE NOUN. Not "The Ford Motor Company is sending their best engineers," but "*its* best engineers." And not "Each of the men and women have to share *their* responsibility," but "Each of the men and women *has* to share *his* or *her* responsibility." See ANTECEDENT; EACH; INDEFINITE PRONOUNS.

Pronunciation has a bearing on spelling, but not because English is phonetic. It is not. Consider the word *forte*. When meaning a strong point, it is pronounced *fort*. But when used as a musical term, it is pronounced *for-tay*. This latter pronunciation could easily cause a misspelling by the unwary. The point being made here is that one should not spell according to sounds. Look the word up in a dictionary. Certainly sound would not lead to the preferred spelling of *schism*, "a separation into opposed groups." It is pronounced *sizm*. The *ch* is silent.

Proper names should be pluralized the same way other nouns are pluralized. The surprising thing is that often an unnecessary apostrophe is added. We should not write *the two Howe's* but *the two Howes.* Just add an *s* or *es* (*Jones, Joneses; Fox, Foxes*), as the case may be. See POSSESSIVES.

Protagonist, an *actor, a leading character in a literary work,* or *a champion of a cause,* is not to be qualified by *chief* or *main.* And it is not to be used in plural form, since there can be only one. Note that *antagonist* seems like an antonym, but it is not. An antagonist is an adversary, one who opposes and actively competes with another.

Provided means *on the condition that* or *understanding that*: "You may enter *provided* you behave yourself." Using *that* is unnecessary after *provided* (*provided that*) unless its omission would cause confusion. The synonym *providing* is often interchanged, but not in the best English, at least in the opinion of some authorities but by no means of all. *Provided,* however, does predominate. And don't forget the simple *if* when it can serve as well as *provided.* In fact, it is sometimes wrong not to use *if.* In "We'll be late for the show *if* we don't hurry," neither *provided* nor *providing* would do.

Public. See COLLECTIVE NOUNS.

Purport, with its sense of *supposed to be,* should be used in the active, not the passive, voice. For example, say, "The document *purports* to contain an authentic signature," not "The document *is purported* to contain an authentic signature."

Q

Quarter to is the correct expression when referring to time, not *a quarter of*.

Question. See AS TO.

Questions that expect an answer should be framed with *shall* or *will* to anticipate the *shall* or *will* in the response: "*Shall* you be attending the next meeting? I *shall* not." "*Will* you sing along with me? Of course I *will*."

You may note that the word *shall* is not in favor with most people. In fact, it is so seldom used that it is believed by many grammarians to be moribund. *Will* has taken over the field and is replacing *shall* in most cases. It seems that the American people have a strong *will*.

Quick/quickly. See REAL.

Quite, in formal English, means *completely*, *totally*, or *entirely* ("He is *quite* right"; "It is *quite* impossible"), and in less formal English, *somewhat* or *rather* ("She is *quite* pretty"; "It is *quite* late"). Avoid using *quite* if the context does not make its meaning clear. For example, what does "It is *quite* satisfactory" mean—*somewhat* or *completely*? Precision is gained if *quite* is replaced by the word that reflects the exact meaning intended.

Quote in formal dialogue is used only as a verb: "You may *quote* me on this." Its noun form is *quotation*. Do not say, "His quote consisted of thirty-three words." Use *quotation* instead.

R

Rack means *to strain with great effort*. **Wrack** means *to destroy* (the storm-*wracked* village), but it is a word for which there is little use. To play it safe, discard *wrack* for *rack* in all its idiomatic senses: *nerve-racking, storm-racked, rack and ruin*. But note that the last expression is sometimes seen spelled *wrack and ruin*, a redundancy and a cliché.

Rapt. See WRAPPED.

Reaction is a term often inaccurately used. A *reaction* is a *spontaneous or an automatic response*, and it is therefore not a proper substitute for *answer, impression, feeling, opinion, reply,* or *response*, any of which requires some thought.

Read where. See SAW WHERE.

Real is an adjective meaning *true, actual,* or *genuine*: "It is a *real* copperhead," meaning a genuine copperhead. **Really** is an adverb: "He is a *really* good boy." Therefore do not say, "We had a real fine meal" or "Frank is real clever." Use *really* or *very* instead. And not "I feel real good today" and not "The shoreline is real clean now," but *really* in both instances. Adverbs, not adjectives, modify adjectives. See ADVERBS; SLOW; VERY.

135

Really. See ADVERBS; REAL.

Reason is because. See REASON.

Recollect/remember are not synonyms, since the process of bringing into memory works differently with each one. A person *recollects* by making a conscious effort to bring to the surface that which has been stored in memory. The process is never instantaneous and is often frustrating. *To remember* is *to recall with little conscious effort.*

Recommended is a word that is not only often misused but also frequently misspelled. If a plumber asks his customer, "Who *recommended* you to me?" we must hope he knows his plumbing better than his English. He should have asked, "Who *referred* you to me?" It was the plumber who was recommended, not the customer. An expert is recommended. A customer, a patient, or a client who seeks advice or help is *referred.*

Redundancy is *superfluous repetition,* or, to put it another way, *words unnecessary to the meaning.* It should be scrupulously avoided, for redundancy is evidence of an incomplete control of the language.

Almost everyone would agree that *free gift* is redundant, as are *new innovation, exact same,* and *hollow tube.* And since a fact, by definition, is true, adding *true* to *facts* creates a redundancy. But be aware that some combinations are so welded that even educated people use them, which means that, although their use is not necessarily recommended here, they should not be criticized. Such phrases as *old adage, endorse on the back,* and *mental telepathy* (*telepathy* is a form of mental communication) have found a comfortable niche for themselves in English.

The best advice on this point comes from William Strunk: "Vigorous writing is concise. A sentence should contain no unnecessary words, a paragraph no unnecessary sentences, for the same reason that a drawing should have no unnecessary lines and a machine no unnecessary parts."

Refer. See ALLUDE.

Referred to. See HYPHENS.

Reflexive pronouns (the *-self* pronouns—*myself, himself, ourselves,* etc.) turn the action back on the subject: "I shave *myself*"; "Howard loves *himself*"; "They named *themselves* guardians of the children." These *-self* pronouns also serve to emphasize or to intensify: "The leading lady *herself* will attend"; "We residents *ourselves* are to blame."

The *-self* pronouns should not be used needlessly for *I, me, us,* and so on. They therefore should not serve as subject or object. Be careful. "Jane and ourselves will go" should be rewritten "Jane and *we.*" And not "Send the bill to Paul and myself," but to "Paul and *me.*" The frequently heard "This is just between you and myself" is an inelegant way of referring to yourself. Say "between you and *me.*" Prepositions, of which *between* is one, take pronouns in the objective case.

Do not surround reflexive pronouns with commas. Not "I, myself, did it." See BETWEEN.

Regard may mean consider, and it then should be used with the preposition *as*. The oddity is that CONSIDER, in the sense of *regard*, is not used with *as*. We may say, "We regard it *as* libelous," or "We consider it libelous" (no *as*).

Do not follow *regard* with an infinitive. Not "The treasurer regards it to be a serious mistake." Substitute *as* for *to be* (*regards it as*).

Regretfully/regrettably are sometimes misused each for the other, even by the educated. *Regretfully* refers to *a person who has feelings of regret*: "*Regretfully*, she severed their relationship." *Regrettably* (two *t*'s) means *unfortunately*: "*Regrettably* they could not attend their son's graduation." Therefore (applying the adjective forms), "The hurricane that upset their cruise plans was *regrettable*," not *regretful*. See HOPEFULLY.

Remainder. See BALANCE.

Remember. See RECOLLECT.

Replace. See SUBSTITUTE.

Reputation. See CHARACTER.

Respectively is a word that does not belong in the complimentary closing of a letter. Not "Respectively yours." *Respectively* refers to a series of items taken in regular order. The word called for in the closing is "*Respectfully*," which means that the writer has respect for the addressee. Another similar-sounding word, one that could cause confusion, is *respectably*. It means *in a manner worthy* *of respect*: "His dissertation was *respectably* presented."

Rest. See BALANCE.

Restrictive/nonrestrictive clauses are mentioned a number of times throughout this book. A *restrictive clause* is one necessary to the sense of the sentence. It may not be omitted and is not surrounded by commas. A *nonrestrictive clause* is its opposite. The information it contains, though interesting, is nevertheless nonessential and may therefore be omitted without harming the sentence. It is surrounded by commas. Note the differences in sense and punctuation in the following: "The brownstone, *which* I lived in for three years, is to be torn down," and "The brownstone *that* I lived in is to be torn down." The first, with the *which*, contains nonessential information. The sentence could survive even if the clause were omitted. But the second, with *that*, needs the clause because it points to the particular brownstone that is to be torn down—the one I lived in. The *nonrestrictive clause* is surrounded by commas. The *restrictive clause* has none. See THAT/WHICH; WHO.

Rout and **Route** cause problems in pronunciation. A *rout*, an *overwhelming defeat*, is pronounced to rhyme with *out*. A *route*, a *road, course*, or *way*, rhymes with *root*.

Robber/thief/burglar are what people are called who unlawfully take something that doesn't belong to them. A *robber* steals by using threats or violence. A *thief* steals secretly or stealthily. A *burglar* enters the premises with felonious intent.

In terms of verbs, a robber robs; a thief steals; but what does a burglar do—*burgle* or *burglarize*? The accepted form today is *burglarize*. *Burgle* is a back-formation regarded as informal.

Note that what a robber takes—money, jewelry, and so on—is *stolen*, not *robbed*. It is incorrect to say, "He is the man who robbed the money."

Run is not an acceptable replacement for *manage* or *operate* where a respectable business is concerned. A person might say, "My bookie joint is *run* by my neighbor," but "My cousin *manages* a shoe store" and "My uncle *operates* three dress shops."

S

Same. See SIMILAR.

Savings is a plural noun. Therefore, "Canceling his subscriptions meant *a savings* of $175 a year" needs to have the *a* omitted to enable *savings* to function correctly as a plural.

Saw where is a disapproved combination. Rather than "I saw on television where the President will return soon," make it "I saw on television *that.* . . ." The expression *read where* is equally objectionable. Do not say, "I read where an economic recession is heading our way." Here again, use *that*: "I read *that.* . . ."

Scan is a word to look at carefully because it has two meanings, each opposite to the other. One is *to examine thoroughly*; the other is *to look over hastily*. A person who scans his income tax return does so painstakingly. A person who scans the newspaper headlines while stopped at a traffic light, or a driver who scans the headline of the newspaper held up by a newsboy, does so quickly.

Be equally careful of *cleave*, which means *to separate*, as to *cleave* a plank in two, and quite oppositely, *to adhere*, as to be glued as person's clothing when one has been caught in a thunderstorm.

Scarcely. See BARELY, HARDLY, SCARCELY.

Seasonable/seasonal both refer to a season. *Seasonable* has a wider usage. In addition to meaning *appropriate to a season* ("Snowy weather is *seasonable* here in January"), it also means *suitable to the circumstances*; that is, coming at the right time ("The bathing suits were a *seasonable* delivery"). The sense of *seasonal* is *pertaining to a season* (*seasonal* employment, *seasonal* allergies).

Seeing as how. See BEING AS.

Seldom ever contains a needless word: *ever*. Say, "He seldom arrives promptly," not "He *seldom ever* arrives promptly."

Semicolon. Although this book does not delve into punctuation, the semicolon merits attention because some writers are unsure when to use it.

In the main, use it to separate independent clauses (those that can stand by themselves) that have no coordinating conjunction between them: "The umpire blew his whistle; the players trotted onto the field." Its second most important use is to follow a clause that is followed by another clause beginning with a conjunctive adverb, such as *therefore, however, accordingly, besides,* and *also*: "We have many financial problems; *nevertheless,* we'll carry on"; "The secretary expects to hear from you by next week; *otherwise,* he'll strike your name"; "I've written you three times; *yet* I have not had a reply."

Furthermore, use the semicolon to separate units in a series that has internal commas: "The speakers include R. C. Brownstein, Omaha; L. R. Smythe, Dallas; and S. B. Walker, Philadelphia." Likewise, in long sentences with internal punctuation, use it to separate a second independent clause, even though it begins with a coordinating conjunction: "The day began with rainfall, became damp and murky, and then baked us to the marrow; *and* we fidgeted from the intense heat and the assault of mosquitoes." See CONJUNCTIVE ADVERBS.

Send. See INDIRECT OBJECTS.

Sensual/sensuous are confusing words because they look so much alike. *Sensual*, which means *appealing to the senses*, has an unfavorable connotation. It refers to physical pleasures, the grosser ones, especially sexual (a mnemonic aid is to note that both *sensual* and *sexual* end in *-ual*). *Sensuous* also means *appealing to the senses*, but it pertains to intellectual pleasures or aesthetic pursuits—art, music, literature—those experienced through all the senses.

Sensuous. See SENSUAL/SENSUOUS.

Sentence. A sentence is a *simple* sentence if it has one subject and one predicate—"Thomas [subject] always sleeps late [predicate]," even if the subject or the predicate consists of compounds: "*Walt* and *Bill* have been *working* and *playing* together." A *compound* sentence is one that contains two or more INDEPENDENT CLAUSES: "The man went home, and the boy left for camp." Note that a comma separates independent clauses and that these clauses are in effect simple sentences that have been joined. A *complex* sentence consists of an independent clause and one or more SUBORDI-NATE CLAUSES: "The zoo keeper cleaned the cage [independent clause], after which he turned his hose on the animals [subordinate clause]."

Sequence of tenses, if properly given, keeps the time expressed in proper order. We say, "I *know* he *is* here," but "I *knew* he *was* there," the tense in the subordinate clause ("he *is* here" and "he *was* there") taking the same tense as that in the main clause ("I *know*" and "I *knew*"). This rule is not followed in a quotation—"They *shouted* [past tense], 'Tom *is* [present tense] a traitor' "—or in a parenthetical expression: "I *realized* then, even as I *do* now, that I *was* wrong." See GENERAL TRUTHS; MIXED TENSES; TENSES; VERBS.

Serious/seriously. See ADVERBS.

Set is a TRANSITIVE VERB. That means it must take an object. It does this by conveying action from the subject to the predicate. You *set* a vase down, you *set* the table, you *set* the stage for a presentation. Some exceptions are "the sun *sets*" and "the hen *sets*." Otherwise, be sure to follow with an object. And do not say, "Sit the vase down." Say "*Set* it [or *put* it] down."

Several. See INDEFINITE PRONOUNS.

Sexism in language has become a driving force in the feminist movement and a bugbear for some writers. The problem may be summed up in this sentence: "Each writer must decide for *himself* how much time *he* should devote to *his* writing." Is the sentence satisfactory as written, or should the sexist words be diluted by saying *himself or herself*, *he or she*, and *his or her*? Or would it be preferable to restructure by using *oneself*, *one*, and *one's*: "Each writer must decide for *oneself* how much time *one* should devote to *one's writing*"?

The sexually diluted phrases sound clumsy to many ears. The impersonal ONE is similarly awkward, even though grammatically correct. The easiest and the most obvious way to unruffle feminine feathers is to use plural forms: "*Writers* must decide for *themselves* how much time *they* should devote to *their* writing." Or, if the work is informal, *you* will resolve the problem: "*You* must decide for *yourself* how much time to devote to *your* writing."

Coming back to the original example, the sentence could have been structured in the singular without offense to anyone: "Each writer must decide how much time to devote to writing." See EVERY.

Shall is obsolescent. Few people, including some of the most educated, use it. *Will* has taken over the field. But no one can fault the traditional use of these auxiliaries: *shall* in the first person to express futurity and *will* in the second and third persons; and the reverse of the formulas to express determination, obligation, willingness, or permission: *will* in the first person and *shall* in the other two persons. To avoid criticism from any source, stay with tradition—if possible.

Remember that if you want to express determination and are not sure whether to use *shall* or *will*,

use *have to* or *must.* You will not go wrong. See
MIXED TENSES.

Should. See MIXED TENSES.

Similar is an adjective, not an adverb. Therefore do
not say, "This machine operates similar to mine,"
but *"similarly* to mine." You may say, "This machine seems *similar* to mine," since *seems* is a
LINKING VERB and is properly followed by an adjective (called a *predicate adjective*), or "The seam-
stress has a *similar* machine" (called an *attributive
adjective*).

Because *similar* connotes a *resemblance,* whereas
same means *identical,* do not interchange these
two. Avoid "Mr. Prescott died last year at sea, and
his son met a similar fate two weeks ago." Make
it *the same fate.*

Since, when expressing time, requires a perfect
tense, not a past tense. Instead of "Joe did not return since he left home last year," say, "Joe *has
not returned* since he left home last year."

Consider this sentence: "As Rose was leaving,
Mabel began to cry." The sentence is imprecise. If
the *reason* for the crying was Rose's leaving, change
as to "Since [or *because*] Rose was leaving, Mabel
began to cry." If the intended sense, however, was
at the time of Rose's leaving, change it to "*While*
Rose was leaving...." One more: "*Since* I lost my
job, I have learned the rigors of the unemployment
line." Does that mean "*because* I lost my job" or
"*from the time* I lost my job"? *Since* can clarify or
create ambiguity. Be careful. See AGO; BECAUSE;

BEING AS/BEING THAT/BEING AS HOW; ELLIPTICAL CLAUSES OF COMPARISON; OMISSION OF WORDS.

Singular and plural nouns must take verbs appropriate to their number. Be alert to the verb required where the noun is always singular (*news, measles, summons*), always plural (*clothes, goods, pants, pliers, premises, thanks*), or sometimes one and sometimes the other (*deer, fish, moose*). Some words are singular or plural depending on the number of the noun in a phrase following *of*: "The politics of our *senator is* motivated by vote-getting"; "The politics of the *communists have* undergone a change."

Note that a plural noun—"The width of the house spans sixteen *feet*"—may become a singular adjective: "The house has a sixteen-*foot* frontage." See COLLECTIVE NOUNS; -ICS; VERBS.

Sink has two past tenses: *sank* and *sunk*. Sank is preferred. *Sunk* functions best as a past participle and *sank* as a past tense. Rather than "The enemy *sunk* two of our ships," prefer "*sank* two of our ships" or the past participle form: "The enemy *has sunk* two of our ships." And do not say that a ship "foundered and sank." *To founder* is *to sink*. Avoid the redundancy by using either *foundered* or *sank*, but not both.

Size is a noun; **sized,** an adjective. You may form a compound adjective with either *size* or *sized: a small-size room* or *a small-sized room; different-size sofas* or *different-sized sofas*. Prefer *sized* to *size* because *sized* in these phrases sounds more formal.

Two things to be aware of. Since *size* is a noun,

it must be followed by *of* when preceding another noun. Not "We want that size printing press," but "that size *of* printing press." The adjective form *sizable* is preferably spelled this way, with no internal *e* (not *sizeable*).

One thing more: Don't use *in size* when it is unnecessary. Write, "The suitcases are large," not large in size.

Slander. See LIBEL.

Slow is both an adjective ("He is a *slow* walker") and an adverb ("What *slow*-moving traffic!"). In formal English the form *slowly*—with its distinctive adverbial ending of *-ly*—predominates. (The adverbs with *-ly* endings are generally preferred to the adjective-adverb.)

Slow is more often seen on highway signs than *slowly* only because *slow* is the shorter and the more vigorous word: "Drive slow." See REAL.

Smell bad, badly. See COPULATIVE VERBS.

So may be used alone when it substitutes for an entire clause: "My husband promises we will travel soon; at least I hope *so*." Although often used as a conjunction to express consequence or result, it is preferable to use a stronger word. For example, rather than "The plans were four months in the making; *so* [*as a result*] we hope everyone will be satisfied," consider ". . . *therefore*, we hope everyone will be satisfied" or ". . . *accordingly* [or *consequently*], we hope everyone will be satisfied."

The approved combination *so that*, to express result, will not steer anyone wrong: "We studied hard all weekend *so that* we could have some free time to play tennis." See AS . . . AS/SO . . . AS; SUCH.

So . . . as. See AS . . . AS/SO . . . AS.

So-called. See HYPHENS.

Some. See ABOUT; INDEFINITE PRONOUNS.

Some day. See SOMETIME.

Someplace. See ANYPLACE.

Sometime is an adverb. **Some time** is an adjective and noun combination. If the expression can be omitted without seriously affecting the sense of the sentence, the word to use is the one-word *sometime.* Without the two-word *some time* a sentence has no meaning. For example, in "Set aside *some time* for me," if *some time* had been omitted ("Set aside . . . for me"), the sentence would have made no sense. But *sometime* may be omitted in "My uncle said he will see my cousins *sometime* soon."

These guidelines also apply to SOMEDAY and SOME DAY.

Somewhere/somewheres. See ANYPLACE.

Sooner is the comparative degree of the adverb *soon.* It should therefore be followed by *than*, not *when.* We say, "Tom is taller *than* Bill" and "Susan is prettier *than* Betty." To be correct we must also say, "No *sooner* had the fly hit the water *than* a trout nipped it." Since both *soon* and *when* suggest time, it seems natural to some writers to use *when* after *soon* or *sooner.* They shouldn't. Idiom calls for *than.*

Sort. See KIND.

Spelling problems ordinarily do not belong in a book on grammar, since orthography is a field of its own. However, a few helpful hints never hurt. In fact, they may do some good.

In the English language only *supersede* has this distinctive spelling of the root word—*sede*. Three words—*exceed, proceed, succeed*—are spelled as given, ending in *-ceed*. All the others with endings that sound alike are spelled *-cede: accede, concede, recede, secede,* and so on.

The *-ery/-ary* words are a source of frustration. Only six important ones end in *-ery: cemetery, confectionery, distillery, millinery, monastery,* and *stationery* (writing material).

It is British, not American, style to double the final *l* before a suffix. The spelling preference in America is *canceled; canceling; traveled; traveling;* and not *cancelled,* and so forth. And note that *marshal* as either noun or verb should be spelled with only one *l*: not *marshall* (noun) and *marshalled* (verb), but *marshal* and *marshaled.*

Words ending in *-like* are written solid (*catlike, childlike, ladylike*), unless the first part ends in *l* (*bell-like, cell-like, girl-like*).

Avoid the spellings *judgement* and *acknowledgement.* Prefer *judgment* and *acknowledgment* (no *e* after the *g*).

With words ending in *-er* or *-re,* prefer *-er* (*center, theater*). Use *-re* only if it is a part of an established name: "Ford's Theatre." By and large in America *-er* is preferred; in Britain, *-re.*

The *i* before *e* rule has served usefully through the years. But be aware of its many exceptions.

Generally, words pronounced with the *ee* sound follow the rule. This means that *ie* rather than *ei* should be used (*believe, wield*) except after *c* (*receive, conceive*).

A last alert, simply because these two words are frequently misspelled. The first is *sacrilegious*. The common error is to spell it *sacreligious*. The second is *pharaoh*. Some people can't find this word in the dictionary because they don't realize that it ends in *aoh*.

Spill. See POUR/SPILL.

Split infinitives (inserting an adverb between the *to* and the verb) do not bother most grammarians anymore. The recommendation, nevertheless, is not to split needlessly, because a split may make for awkwardness. This is especially true when a long intervening series of words between the *to* and the verb form distorts the sentence: "After regaining consciousness, he was able to, although he had trouble in distinguishing objects, make his presence known." It would be better to place the intervening words after *consciousness*.

But if euphony, emphasis, or common sense seems to applaud a split, split. Do not hesitate to say, "to openly admit," "to strongly criticize," "to really believe," "to thoroughly understand," "to so arrange." The split infinitive is no longer the bugbear it used to be. See INFINITIVES.

Spoonfuls. See -FUL.

Squinting modifiers are so placed that they become, like Janus, two-faced, looking in opposite directions at the same time. They are therefore ambiguously positioned. In "She told him this morning she was leaving," one may wonder whether she told him this morning or whether she was leaving this morning. Or consider, "His smiling constantly upset the audience." We cannot tell whether he was smiling constantly or whether the audience was constantly upset. One more: "The doctor said that if we did not take our tick-ridden German shepherd to a colder climate within a year the dog would die." Question: Must we move within a year, or would the dog be dead within a year?

What is clear is that squinting modifiers must be avoided for the sake of clarity. Going back to the first example and rephrasing, we might arrive at: "She told him this morning that she was leaving" or "She told him that she would be leaving this morning."

Stalactite will always be spelled correctly if you bear in mind that this form of congealed water resembling an icicle hangs from the ceiling and has a *c* for *ceiling* within it. Its counterpart, **stalagmite**, which rises from the ground, has a *g* for *ground* within it.

Start. See BEGIN.

Stationary means *not moving* or *fixed in place*. **Stationery** is *writing material*. Note the *e* in *stationery*. Let *letters* and *envelopes* (with their *e*'s) remind you of the *e* in *stationery*. See SPELLING.

Still. See AS YET.

Subject of a sentence: It governs the *number* (whether singular or plural) and *person* (whether first, second, or third) of the verb. In "The *boy plays* well," the subject *boy* is singular and so is the verb *plays*. In "The *boys play* well," both subject and verb are plural.

Those examples raise no problems, and the principles involved are clear. But care must be exercised with other constructions; for example, such sentences as "The carton of cigarettes I bought are on the kitchen table" and "A quartet of young men from Boston are to entertain." The subjects are singular (*carton, quartet*) but the plurals *cigarettes* and *men* tend to mislead. Those plurals are objects of the preposition *of* and have no bearing on the number of the subject. The verb *are* in each case should be changed to *is* to make the verb agree with its singular subject.

One more, but this one a change from *is* to *are*: "His recent successes is the result of his unflagging drive." The subject is the plural *successes*, which requires the plural verb form *are*.

Still more: The rule is that the object of a prepositional phrase beginning with *of* that follows *a fraction, most, some,* or *rest* (words denoting a part or a portion) governs the number of the verb. This is the reverse of what was said in the *carton* and *quartet* examples previously discussed. But the rule applicable here, as was just pointed out, involves *of* phrases that denote a part or portion. Hence "A half of the *manuscript has been* completed," but "A half of the *employees are* on vacation." "The rest of the *book is* unadulterated trash," but "I'm glad that the rest of the *pages are* water soaked." See AND; PREDICATE NOMINATIVE; VERB; THERE.

Subjunctive mood. See MOOD.

Subordinate clause—*a group of words that has a subject and a predicate but cannot stand alone because it does not constitute a complete sentence.* For example, in "We entered the courtroom as the lawyer was speaking," "We entered the courtroom" can stand by itself. It is an independent clause and could be followed by a period. But "as the lawyer was speaking" cannot stand alone. It is grammatically incomplete. Such clauses are sometimes called *dependent clauses* because their use depends on an independent clause, without which their use would be illogical. Note that subordinate clauses are introduced by subordinating conjunctions: *after, although, as, because, before, even if, even though, except, if, in order that, provided, since, so that, than, that, till, though, unless, until, when, where, whether, while.* Let one of these little words alert you to a possible subordinate clause.

Subordinating conjunctions. See SUBORDINATE CLAUSE.

Substitute/replace are said to be synonyms, but they are far from exact synonyms, even though a replacement and a substitution may wind up with the same result.

To substitute is *to put in the place of.* *To replace* is *to take the place of.* If a red book is removed from the desk and a brown one is put in its place, the brown book has been substituted for the red one and the red book has been replaced by the brown.

Each of these words takes its own preposition. *Substitute* takes *for* and *replace* takes *by* or *with*.

Successfully is unnecessary baggage when other words in the sentence indicate success. For example, the sentence "The pharmaceutical company has successfully developed a vaccine to protect our troops from the effects of biological weapons" needs to have the *successfully* deleted. You can't develop something unsuccessfully.

Such is not the equivalent of *this*. In "David, our nominee, is *such* a man," the sense is *a man of that sort*. In "*This* is our nominee," the sense is *the man just mentioned*. In "He would read histories and biographies, but even *such* books did not quench his thirst for knowledge," *these* should replace *such*.

Informally *such* may be used as an intensifier: "It was *such* a hot day." In better speech and writing the sense must be completed; for example, "It was *such* a hot day that we had to retreat to our air-conditioned house." Other words often used as informal intensifiers are *so* and *that*: "I was *so* tired" (which doesn't tell us what happened as a result of the tiredness); "I didn't believe it would be *that* cold" (to prevent what activity?).

Such a is the correct formula before a singular countable noun: "*Such a* person is worth waiting for." But in a negative construction *a* is omitted: "No *such* person will be admitted" (no *a*).

Such a. See MANY A; SUCH.

Such . . . as is a correct combination. Avoid *such . . . that* and *such . . . who*. Not "We own such mowers that are needed by the city," but "We own *such* mowers *as* are needed by the city." And not "I would like to know such people who are interested in the theater," but "I would like to know *such* people *as* are interested in the theater."

One exception. *That* may be used where *result* is indicated: "He works *such* long hours *that* he seldom sees his family."

Such as . . . and others do not belong together. Use one or the other. Either "Ball players *such as* Lou Gehrig and Babe Ruth are . . ." or "Lou Gehrig, Babe Ruth, *and other* ball players are . . ." but not "Ball players such as Lou Gehrig, Babe Ruth, *and others* are. . . ."

Summons. See SINGULAR AND PLURAL NOUNS.

Superior to is the correct idiom, not *superior than*.

Superlative forms of adjectives compare more than two persons or things: "He is the *best* student we have." However, we must be aware of idioms such as "Put your *best* foot forward" (we have only two feet). And it is not unusual to hear someone say, during an election campaign in which there are only two candidates: "May the *best* man win."

Neither *else* nor *other* is used with a superlative. Correctly put: "Oregon has the most trees *of any state* in the union," not "of any *other* state in the union." See COMPARATIVE FORMS.

Surprised, meaning *taken unaware*, is followed by the preposition *by* ("My daughter was *surprised by* my unexpected appearance"). When the sense is *amazed, surprised* takes *at* ("We were all *surprised at* his lack of understanding") or an infinitive ("My daughter was *surprised to see* me") or *that* ("My daughter was *surprised that* I was there").

T

Take. See BRING.

Target, meaning *to aim, to aspire to,* is a good crisp verb that, although objected to by some critics, is approved of by others. Do not hesitate to use it, but sparingly: "We will *target* our sales this fall toward the young adult."

Team. See COLLECTIVE NOUNS.

Tense (meaning *time*) indicates the relative time when action is taking place, took place, or will take place. The *present perfect tense,* which always uses the auxiliary *has* or *have,* brings past action into the present: "William *has run* out of gas"; "Murray *has earned* a promotion." The *past perfect tense* indicates an action completed before another action in past time: "The vendor *had sold* [past perfect tense] all his beer before I approached [past tense] him"; "The student *had finished* [past perfect tense] typing before the machine broke [past tense]."

A caution: Avoid "Malcolm would have given away any sum to have been chosen." Make it "Malcolm would have given away any sum *to be chosen.*" And not "Seymour would have been glad *to have flown home,*" but *"to fly home."*

158

Afterthought: If the verb in the main clause is in the past tense, usually the verb in the subordinate clause will follow suit. It too will be in the past tense. This rule is best understood through examples: "I *heard* that he *was* here" (even though he is still here). "Jim testified that he *lived* in Trenton" (although he still lives there). See GENERAL TRUTHS; MIXED TENSES; SEQUENCE OF TENSES; VERBS.

Than, when used to make comparisons, is followed by a pronoun in the nominative case (*I, he, we*) if a verb concept follows it. For example, "He is taller than *I*" ("... am tall" is understood). "They have more money than *we*" ("... have" is understood). But note the distinctions in the next two examples: "Mary likes John more than *me*" ("more than she likes me"); "Mary likes John more than *I*" ("more than I like John"). The guideline to follow: The case of the pronoun after *than* is that which would be used if the sentence were written out more fully. See AS; BARELY/HARDLY/SCARCELY; COMPARATIVE FORMS OF ADJECTIVES.

Thanks. See SINGULAR AND PLURAL NOUNS.

That, serving as a relative pronoun, introduces RESTRICTIVE CLAUSES, those necessary to the sense of a sentence: "This is the racing car *that* won the race." **Which** is used to introduce *nonrestrictive clauses*, those that are not essential to the meaning of the sentence and that can be omitted without harm: "This racing car, *which* my uncle bought last month, won the race." Note that the *which* clause is surrounded by commas. The *that* clause has none.

When *that* is used as a conjunction, it may be omitted except in strict formal writing: "I was so exhausted [no *that*] I could hardly stand up"; "I knew [no *that*] he was going bankrupt."

Be on guard for verb agreement with the pronoun *that*. In "It is one of the most successful plays that *has* been on Broadway," *has* must be changed to *have*, since the verb has to agree in number with the antecedent of *that*, which is plural: "plays that have." See DOUBT; OMISSION OF WORDS; ONE OF THE; SO; SUCH; SUCH . . . AS; WHO.

That is introduces an *explanation*, an *enumeration*, or a *list*. Although the phrase is always followed by a comma, the punctuation mark that precedes it may be a semicolon ("The colors available are the primary ones; that is, red, blue, and yellow"); or a comma ("The temperature was high, that is, ninety-two degrees"); or a dash ("We traveled alone— that is, we didn't take our guide along").

These punctuation marks may also be used with *for example*, *for instance*, and *namely*.

The should be repeated when two or more adjectives pertain to different nouns—"He chose *the* navy suit and *the* beige suit" (two suits)—but not when they modify the same noun: "He chose *the* navy and beige necktie" (one necktie). And so with "We heard from *the* secretary and treasurer," which pertains to one person; "*the* secretary and *the* treasurer" pertains to two.

If two or more adjectives modify a singular noun, use *the* before *each* adjective—"Here are *the* first and *the* second copy"—but *the* only before the *first* adjective if the noun is plural: "Here are *the* first and [no *the*] second copies."

It is optional, but preferable, to omit *the* when it is part of a proper name and preceded by a possessive form, as in "Here is his *New York Times*" (rather than "his *The New York Times*") and "I have recently read Shakespeare's *Tempest*" (rather than "read Shakespeare's *The Tempest*"). See A; OMISSIONS.

Then (an adverb of time) is properly used in a sentence such as "I knew the *then* chairman." However, it should be borne in mind that not all authorities approve of this usage.

If *then* is used as a conjunctive adverb (joining two independent clauses with no coordinating conjunction between them), a semicolon between the clauses is usually better than a comma: "We rushed back to lock up the house; *then* we left." But if *and* precedes *then*, a comma should be used instead. See CONJUNCTIVE ADVERBS.

There is/there are (called *anticipatory subjects*—see IT) is followed by a verb that agrees with the true subject, as in "*There is* a large *oak* on my lawn, and *there are* many *bushes* nearby." Test it by inversion, "A large *oak* is on my lawn" (no *there*). "Many *bushes* are nearby" (no *there*). Some writers use *there is* to introduce a compound subject if the first item is singular, the theory being that the singular initial item attracts a singular verb—*is*: "There *is* a pencil, two pens, an eraser, and a ruler on my desk." Others would opt for the plural *are*.

What has been said about the introductory *there*

applies to the introductory *here*: "Here *is* an apple"; "Here *are* two apples."

Thief. See ROBBER/THIEF/BURGLAR.

Though. See ALTHOUGH.

Through. See FINISHED.

Till/until are equally acceptable terms in any form of speech or writing. They may be used as a preposition—"We'll be gone *till* [or *until*] Wednesday"— or as a conjunction—"We'll wait *until* [or *till*] they arrive."

Avoid the clipped form *'til*.

Time. See A.M./P.M.

Titles of books and works of art take a singular verb, even when the title is in a plural form ("*The Canterbury Tales was* one of the earliest books written in English"). Treat the names of organizations and countries the same way ("The United States *is* one great country"). But be careful of exceptions established by usage: "The Phillies *are* a formidable team." See DOUBLE TITLING.

To be, the commonest verb in the English language, takes the same case after it as it did before it. Therefore, to the question "Who's there?" the reply, strictly speaking, should be "It is I." But "It's me" is so often used that it has attained idiomatic credentials. The feeling of many grammarians is that since the pronoun comes after the verb, it is, so to speak, in "object territory," which makes *me* in "It's *me*" acceptable. See ABLE TO; ME.

Together with. See PARENTHETICAL ELEMENTS.

Too is usually set off by commas when it appears at or near the end of a sentence—"Sydney will be going with us, *too*"—but not so frequently when it appears toward the beginning—"Herb *too* will be joining us." Beware, however, of such a sentence as "Sam, *too*, often likes to be with us." Without the commas the sentence might be taken to mean that Sam likes to be with us *too much*. See PAST PARTI-CIPLES.

A total of . . . were/the total of . . . was is a choice that confounds some writers. The answer is that the *a* takes a plural verb and the *the* takes a singular. These idiomatic formulas are the same as those applied to the word NUMBER. Incidentally, the phrase "a total of" is often surplusage. For example, "There were *a total of* forty-six members at the meeting" would be improved by the excision of *a total of*: "There were forty-six members at the meeting."

Toward/towards (as well as **onward/onwards, backward/backwards**) are equally acceptable according to most dictionaries. Regardless, it is preferable to omit the final *s*.

Transition, *in grammar,* is *the passing of thoughts from one to another so that they are tied together and are readily understood.* The simplest way to do this is by inserting a word or phrase—a *connective*—to carry the reader across. Common connectives are *therefore, however, on the other hand, for this reason, equally important,* and *finally.* Without the proper use of connectives, sentences sound disjointed and choppy. See CONJUNCTIVE ADVERBS.

Transitive verbs, those that take an object ("I buy a *paper* daily"), may take both a DIRECT OBJECT and an indirect object. An INDIRECT OBJECT that precedes a direct object, its sense being *to whom* or *for whom*, is used particularly after the verbs *get, give, lend, offer, read, send, show, tell, buy, pay,* and *write*: "My father paid the *bank* [indirect object] the full *amount* of the loan [direct object]"; "I gave *Jane* [indirect object] the *books* [direct object]"; "My mother wrote the *principal* [indirect object] a nice *letter* [direct object]." See INTRANSITIVE VERBS.

Transpire is a word that sounds elegant to those who shun plain English. But the word is misused more often than it is used correctly. *To transpire* is *to leak out* or *become known*. It does not mean to occur or to happen. Something that transpired in 1990 may have occurred many years before. This means that one should not say, for example, "After four months had transpired, he finally got an answer." Make it "After four months had *elapsed* [or *passed*]. . . ." Be cautious. If you're not sure whether you're using the word properly, switch to one you're sure of.

True facts is a redundant phrase. Delete *true*. A fact could not be one if it were not true.

Try and. See AND.

Type. See DOUBLE PREPOSITIONS.

U

Unbelievable. See ADJECTIVES.

Under pertains to direction, not to number. Therefore do not say, "There were *under* forty men at the meeting" or "It weighed *under* fifty pounds." Make it, respectively, *fewer than* and *less than*.

Uninterested. See DISINTERESTED.

Unique means *unequaled, one of a kind*. Since it is an ABSOLUTE TERM, it should not be compared or qualified, which means it should not be preceded by *more* or *most*. Nothing can be *more* unique than something else or the *most* unique of all. Either it's unique or it's not. However, a latitude that enables one to back down a bit is that *almost* or *nearly* may qualify *unique* (or almost any other absolute term).

But if the superlative form *most* is so appealing, try "most unusual," an acceptable combination that says the same thing while bypassing the *unique* problem.

It is best, so as not to disturb the equilibrium of any grammarian, to avoid qualifying *unique*, not only with *more* or *most*, but also with *rather, somewhat,* or *very*. But such words as *certainly, really,* and *perhaps* may serve as qualifiers: "It is

certainly unique"; "The vase is *really* unique." See
ABSOLUTE TERMS.

Unit measurement. See WEIGHTS/MONEY/MEASURE-
MENTS.

Universal truths. See GENERAL TRUTHS.

Unless and until. See CANNOT AND WILL NOT.

Until. See TILL/UNTIL.

Up to date. See HYPHENS.

Use/usage are terms that have the meaning of *ha-
bitual* or *customary practices.* In matters of language, *usage* refers to a standard of use, especially
in the meaning and pronunciation of words. However, in almost all instances outside of references
to language, the term *use* serves adequately, and
perhaps better.

Used is called for, not *use*, in a sentence such as "I
used [not *use*] to go there every Tuesday."

Utilize has several senses, all good and acceptable:
*to use profitably, to make use of something not
designed for the purpose,* or *to make use of something ready to be discarded.* A frequent use, or misuse, however, is to equate it with *use. Utilize* is
not its synonym.

V

Verb—*a word that expresses action or a state of being*, which means that it makes a statement about the subject. For example, "The boy *stole* the candy bar." The word *stole* is an action verb, as are most English verbs. But—and this is an important *but*—some verbs do not express action; they connect, or link, the subject to a noun or adjective in the predicate. For example, "Harmon *is* old," "Her cooking *smells* good," and "My wife's name *is* Mildred." Any form of the verb *to be* or any verb of the senses, such as *smell*, as well as some other verbs, like *grow* or *become*, are called copulative or LINKING VERBS.

Verbs must agree with their subjects in NUMBER—singular or plural—and in PERSON—first, second, third—and *not* with PREDICATE NOMINATIVES. Although the rule sounds simple, its application is sometimes troublesome. For example, it is correct to say, "My brothers *were* the source of my financial support" (plural verb *were* agrees with plural subject *brothers*). But if the sentence is inverted— "The source of my financial support *were* my brothers"—the verb form required to agree with the subject *source* is *was*, a singular verb (*brothers* is now serving as a predicate nominative following the linking verb "to be").

Remember that words intervening between subject and verb do not affect the number of the verb. They should be ignored. Not "The reason for all the desks, books, and supplies *were* increased enrollment," but "The reason . . . *was*." Not "The longest part of the play *were* the third and fifth scenes," but "The longest part . . . *was*." See AND; GENERAL TRUTHS; INTERVENING WORDS OR PHRASES; LINKING VERBS; NEGATIVE AND POSITIVE SUBJECTS; SEQUENCE OF TENSES; SINGULAR AND PLURAL NOUNS; SUBJECT OF A SENTENCE; TENSE.

Verbal. See ORAL/VERBAL.

Very is a word usually employed to emphasize, but in many cases its omission will strengthen a statement, not weaken it. Prefer "He is honest" to "He is *very* honest." *Very* belongs in a retirement home, and should be wheeled out only on rare occasions.

Even worse than the excessive use of *very* is the equating of it with *plenty* ("He is *plenty* sorry) or *awful* or *awfully* ("He is an *awful* nice man"). In those instances, since a writer has his back to the wall and must choose, it is better to take *very*. See PAST PARTICIPLES.

Viable means, traditionally, *able to survive and grow* (a *viable* fetus). But it has been given many new meanings, especially by those who like the pompous sound of the word: *real; workable; vivid; practicable; important; feasible.* Thoughtful users of English, because of these extended, varied definitions, find it best to leave the word alone.

Virtually. See PRACTICALLY.

Voice refers to whether a verb is active or passive.

The *active voice* is the one in which the subject is the doer of the action ("*Tom* threw the ball"). The active voice is vigorous, forceful, and economical. Favor it. In the *passive voice* the subject is acted upon: "The *ball* was thrown by Tom." Note that the object of the active voice (*ball*) became the subject of the passive voice.

Although the passive voice is weaker and less forceful than the active, it is nevertheless useful when the agent of the action is unknown, unimportant, or unidentified ("Unfortunately, a hitchhiker *was tossed* onto the sidewalk by one of our trucks"). The passive voice is formed by combining a form of the verb *to be* with a past participle.

Caveat: Do not mix voices by shifting from active to passive. Instead of "The scouts *considered* the problem for two hours before they *were told* to adjourn," make it "The scouts *considered* the problem for two hours before the scoutmaster *told* them to adjourn."

W

Wait on, as in "We're waiting on my aunt," is dialectal. The correct preposition is *for*: "We're waiting *for* my aunt." However, *wait on* is properly used, and is idiomatic, in "The maître d' in this beautiful restaurant *waits on* his customers promptly."

Was/were. See MOOD.

Was a former is redundant, since both *was* and *former* imply a previous happening. In "Ruth was a former secretary of mine," change *was* to *is* or drop *former*.

Ways, when used for *way*, is substandard. Say, "The school is a long *way* [not *ways*] from here."

Weights/money/measurements, even though the amount is more than one, take a singular verb: "Ten minutes *is* [ten dollars *is*, ten feet *is*, ten pounds *is*]." Of course, a reference to ten individual dollars takes a plural verb: "Here *are* ten new one-dollar bills." But when a number higher than one precedes a noun to form a compound adjective (*a six-minute* interval)—two or more words per adjective—the noun and the verb following are both in the singular: "A ten-minute *discussion is* all we have time for"; "A two-week *vacation is* all we can

170

look forward to." See PLUS; SINGULAR AND PLURAL NOUNS; VERBS.

Well is both an adverb and an adjective. Hence, "He feels *well*" may refer either to his state of health (here *feel* is a linking verb and *well* an adjective) or to his sense of touch (here *feel* is an active verb and *well* an adverb). In comparison with the adjective *good*, *well*, when referring to a person, means *in good health*; *good*, always an adjective, points to a person's *appearance, attire, and general demeanor*. But observe that we say, "He plays *well*" (adverb) and "His playing is *good*" (predicate adjective). See GOOD; LINKING VERBS.

West should be capitalized when it denotes a specific region ("Ivan defected to the *West*"; "My aunt lives in the Far *West*"). Capitalize it also when used as an adjective before a proper noun ("*West* Virginia, *West* Indies"). Otherwise make it lowercase: "We will drive *west* for two hours"; "The *west* side of town is nicer." Of course these conventions apply as well to *east, south,* and *north*.

What should not replace *that* where a clear antecedent has preceded. Therefore, not "This is a matter what should be noted on the record," but "This is a matter *that* should be noted on the record," since *matter* is a clear antecedent. *What* is frequently used as a replacement for *that which*, but it should not be in strict formal prose. Instead of "In order to do what we think proper, we'll argue the point," formalists would prefer "In order to do *that which* we think proper, we will argue the point."

Note the difference in the choice of verbs to modify the subject *what* in the following examples: "What is needed *is* a change"; "What are needed *are* changes." The number in the PREDICATE NOMINATIVE controls. To determine whether *what* is a singular or a plural, ask yourself what *what* stands for—"a thing that" or "things that."

When/where should not introduce a definition. Instead of "A hurricane *is when* a very high wind blows," say, "A hurricane is a violent *storm*." And not "Ignorance *is when* a person doesn't know," but "Ignorance is the *absence* of knowledge." Not "I read *where* a monument for Roosevelt is to be erected," but "I read *that* a monument for Roosevelt is to be erected." Use *when* to indicate time and *where* to indicate location or position. See AT.

Where. See WHEN/WHERE.

Whether may stand alone, that is, without *or not*, if the alternatives are expressed: "*Whether* to open another unit or to close one will be discussed at the next meeting." In such case, *or not* is superfluous. The *or not* is likewise superfluous in "I don't know *whether* I'll stay," since *whether* means "that or not that." Or you may apply the "if" test, which gives a quick answer in many instances. According to this test, *or not* should not follow *whether* when *if* stands for *whether*. In "It is not known whether *or not* the United States favors the move" and in "We were wondering whether *or not* my uncle would attend," *or not* is unnecessary, since *if* could replace *whether*. But in "We're going whether or not it snows," if the intention is to go regardless of the weather, *or not* is essential. Here the *if* test would fail. See DOUBT; IF/WHETHER.

Which. See AND WHICH; THAT.

While. See AS; AWHILE; BECAUSE; SINCE.

Will. See MIXED TENSES; SHALL.

Who, and the clause it heads, may be either necessary or unnecessary to the sense of the sentence, depending on its use. In "The man in the red coat, *who spoke at our luncheon today,* is my next door neighbor," the *who* clause simply adds information without which the sentence can survive. "The man in the red coat is my next door neighbor" is the essence of the sentence. The *who* clause is parenthetical and, in grammar, is said to be *nonrestrictive,* and therefore can be omitted. In "The man *who spoke at our luncheon* is a neighbor," the *who* clause is necessary, that is, it is *restrictive* or essential to the sense of the sentence because it identifies the person, the one who is a neighbor. The neighbor is not any man but the *man who spoke at our luncheon.*

Note that the nonrestrictive clause is surrounded by commas; the restrictive clause is not.

Prefer *who* to *that* when the reference is to a proper noun ("It is John Garvey *who* is standing there") and *that* to a generic person ("A businessman *that* works hard is bound to succeed"). The reference of *who* is only to people. Not "The cat who mauls our pillows is a Siamese," but "The cat *that.* . . ." See THAT; WHOM/WHOMEVER.

Whoever. See WHOM/WHOMEVER.

Whom/whomever are sometimes incorrectly used for *who* and *whoever*. Not "Whom should I say is calling?" And not "Tom knows a man whom he believes is a good mechanic." Use *who* in each example, a nominative-case form serving as the subject of "is calling" and "is a good mechanic." The expressions "should I say" and "he believes" are in effect parenthetic and can be omitted after *who* replaces *whom*. But observe that "Who did you give it to?" is wrong because the preposition *to* requires an objective-case form—*whom*: "Whom did you give it to?" or, restating it in natural order to prove the point, "You did give it *to whom*."

Be not misled into using *whomever* in "Give the balloon to whomever wants it," for the pronoun is the subject of the verb *wants*, not the object of the preposition *to*. Make it "to *whoever* wants it," *whoever* being a nominative-case form, one that a subject requires. Consider another: "Everyone had ideas about *who/whom* should win." The preposition *about* has no bearing on the case of the pronoun. The correct pronoun is *who* because it is the subject of the verb *should win*.

Whom, not *who*, should be used after *than*: "My father, *than whom* no man deserved more praise, was a lovable man."

In informal language *who* predominates over *whom* when the pronoun is in what may be called "subject territory." Thus *who* commonly would be used in "Who did the mayor accuse of lying to him?" In formal language *whom* would be required. See WHO.

Whose, the possessive form for *who* or *which*, traditionally was employed only of animate things, such as people, animals, or plants. The formula used with inanimate objects was *of which*. But no longer. *Whose* is now used in all cases: "The book *whose* pages are torn is my brother's"; "A car *whose* muffler is broken cannot pass inspection."

Caveat: Who's is the contraction of *who is—* "Who's going to drive me home?"—or *who has:* "Who's seen the lunch basket?" Do not confuse with *whose*. Not "Who's car will you be driving?" but "*Whose* car?"

Widow refers to a *surviving female spouse*. It should not be followed by *the late*, as in "Amelia Frey, the widow of the late Burton Frey, will be moving to another town." Drop *the late*.

With. See PARENTHETICAL ELEMENTS.

Would. See MIXED TENSES.

Would of. See OF.

Would have is incorrectly used after *if*, since *if* expresses a condition in the past. Use *had*. Say, "If you *had* told me, I would not have asked," not "If you *would have* told me, I would not have asked." One more: "If I *had* been home earlier, I would have prepared dinner for the family," not "If I *would have* been home earlier, I would have prepared dinner for the family."

Wrack. See RACK.

Wrapped refers to *something enclosed by a wrapper*. We speak of a box wrapped in Christmas paper.

Rapt refers to *a person carried away by* or *absorbed in his thoughts.* Although a person is engrossed or *rapt*, not *wrapped*, in thought, figuratively that person may be said to be all *wrapped up* in classical music.

Write. See INDIRECT OBJECTS.

X

X ray, used as a noun, is written as given, although some stylists would place a hyphen between *X* and *ray*. But most writers who omit the hyphen with the noun use it with the adjective ("an *x-ray* photograph") or the participle ("The boy's leg was *x-rayed*") or a verb ("We'll have to *x-ray* your arm").

Y

Yes (and **no**) needs no quotation marks in a sentence such as "He replied *yes*; he would vote for it."

Yet, in negative sentences in which it is an adverb meaning *up to now*, takes a perfect tense, one with *have* or *had*. Therefore, not "The teacher gave me a book, but I did not open it yet," but "I *have not opened* it *yet*." And not "the architects did not call yet," but "The architects *have not called yet*."

It is best not to tie *as* to *yet* where *yet* alone will suffice. For example, "Caldwell has not as yet made his plans" needs no *as*.

One more caution: As an adverb of time, *yet* may overlap *still*. "Are the Getsons here yet?" may be interpreted to mean either "Have they arrived?" or "Are they *still* here?" A sentence of this kind should be restructured to avoid ambiguity. See BUT.

Your/you're are sometimes confused, possibly because of hasty writing. *Your* means *belonging to you*, and *you're* is a contraction of *you are*.

To show possession in the second person, use *yours*. There's no such word as *your's*. No possessive form of a personal pronoun—*his, hers, theirs,* for example—takes an apostrophe.

Z

Zoom means *to climb steeply*. It is now acceptably used, however, to refer to rapid travel on a level,
horizontally. Beyond that, its use has not moved.
Zoom is not to be equated with *plunge* or *swoop*.
Climb with it, or keep it on the level.

Bibliography

Those who wish to pursue the study of grammar and word usage along avenues wider than those we have strolled down together in the *One-Minute Grammarian* may find the material in the following titles useful and to their liking.

Bernstein, Theodore M., *The Careful Writer*. New York: Atheneum.

Bremner, John B., *Words on Words*. New York: Columbia University Press.

Fowler, H.W., *A Dictionary of Modern English*. London: Oxford University Press.

Freeman, Morton S., *A Handbook of Problem Words & Phrases*. Philadelphia: ISI Press.

————*Words to the Wise*. New York: Meridian/NAL.

Mager, N.H., and S.K. Mager, *Encyclopedic Dictionary of English Usage*. Englewood Cliffs, N.J.: Prentice-Hall.

Safire, William, *On Language*. New York: Avon Books.

————*What's the Good Word?* New York: Times Books.

Strunk, J. William, and E.B. White, *The Elements of Style*. New York: Macmillan.